EVOLUTION &CREATION

A CATHOLIC UNDERSTANDING

Rev. William Kramer, C.PP.S.

Our Sunday Visitor Publishing Division
Our Sunday Visitor, Inc.
Huntington, Indiana 46750

Nihil Obstat:
Rev. Donald J. Tracey
Censor Librorum

Imprimatur:
✠ William L. Higi
Bishop of Lafayette-in-Indiana
April 3, 1986

International Standard Book Number: 0-87973-511-2
Library of Congress Catalog Card Number: 86-60907

Cover design and illustrations by James E. McIlrath

PRINTED IN THE UNITED STATES OF AMERICA

511

Contents

Acknowledgments

Scripture texts contained in this work, unless otherwise noted, are taken from the *Revised Standard Version Bible, Catholic Edition*, © 1965 and 1966 by the Division of Christian Education of the National Council of the Churches of Christ in the U.S.A., and used by permission of the copyright owner. Other sources from which material has been excerpted or has served as the basis for portions of this work are cited in the bibliography. If any copyrighted materials have been inadvertently used in this book without proper credit being given, please notify Our Sunday Visitor in writing so that future printings of this work may be corrected accordingly.

Foreword

A lively debate has taken place in recent years between creationists and evolutionists, especially since the Creation Research Society took up the cause of creationism in 1963. The rash of books, articles, and lawsuits makes it clear that neither side in the controversy has much use for *theistic evolution*, the intermediate position accepted by most Christian authors, including Catholics. Those who hold this moderate position do not of course regard it as a middle-of-the-road compromise, arrived at by measuring off equal distances between the two sides, but as a solidly based position flanked by two shaky extremes.

The reason for taking on both sides at once in a little book like this is not to add fuel to the flames but to offer a few basic thoughts for Catholics who must often live with the two extreme views, which are found not only in the larger society but also among members of the Church. On the one hand there are Catholic creationists who claim that those who hold "continuous creation by evolution" make a god of evolution and sin against the first commandment (Haigh, p. 23*). On the other hand, Catholics educated in

---

*References to sources and to further reading are made not by numbered notes but by the use of last names of the authors (with page numbers and/or titles, dates of publication, and other pertinent data, as needed for identification). These authors are listed alphabetically in the bibliography.

an entirely secular environment may easily come away with the impression that evolution has made creation superfluous. They may live in a limbo of confusion, suffering from a schizophrenic division of the mind between faith and knowledge, between "what the Catholic Church teaches" and what "really is" according to science. The Church therefore has a keen pastoral interest in the controversy.

Three points about the Catholic middle way may be stated at the outset:

1. That God created the universe we know is basic Catholic doctrine. How he did it is not revealed at the level of detail that is of interest to science.

2. The Bible contains no error in what the sacred writer intended to teach. But he presents his message in popular language and stories which reflect the views of the people of the time. God did not correct their views of nature.

3. The Church is entrusted with revealed doctrine on the one hand, and on the other hand respects the autonomy of natural knowledge. Faith and science often touch the same subject, such as the origin of things; but since the source of truth is one, science and faith cannot conflict when properly understood.

From this perspective the book will treat three main topics:

1. Creationism and its fundamentalist antecedents, such as the flat-earth movement. It is the creationist claim that all living species were created separately along with the rest of the universe in a period of six days some six thousand years ago, according to information derived from the Bible. It is the contention of most Christian thinkers that this distorts the sacred writings into a natural science text, which they were not meant to be. It is hoped that an

6

excursion into history will help to show that there is no more basis in Scripture or science for a six-day creation than for a flat earth.

2. Evolution, which is distinguished into evolution as a process of nature, evolution as a scientific theory, and evolution as an ideology. It is the ideological overburden which encroaches on religion.

3. Creation, which even though it stands at the head of the Creed, can be known by reason from the things that are seen.

I hope that by sorting through these ideas within a modest compass, this book may be of some use to students of science, to teachers whose lives revolve around these questions, and to parents who must react wisely when their children come home from school announcing, "The Bible is wrong."

Although I owe a debt of gratitude to many, I would like to give special thanks to Rev. Charles Robbins, C.PP.S., for general advice, to Dr. John Nichols for guidance in philosophy, and to Mr. Michael Davis for consultation on questions of science.

William Kramer, C.PP.S., Sc.D.
St. Joseph's College
Rensselaer, Indiana

1

The Fundamentalist Story

Modern fundamentalism became an organized movement among Protestants in the early twentieth century as a reaction against liberalism. It culminated in the founding of the World's Christian Fundamental Association in 1918. Organization has been fluid, but the movement goes on in many forms, including creationism.

During the same time, the first third of the century, many Catholics reacted to the Modernist threat with a similar kind of exaggerated traditionalism, an "intemperate zeal which imagines that whatever is new should for that reason be opposed or suspect" (Pope Pius XII, *Divino Afflante Spiritu*, No. 47).

The principal danger in listening to fundamentalists

lies not so much in their occasional criticism of the Church (see Peter Stravinskas for *The Catholic Response* to this criticism) but in their comfortable certitudes that lure Catholics from the living voice of the Church. Christ promised (see John 16:13) that the Spirit guiding the Church would be faithful to tradition, speaking only what he hears, what is Christ's. But Christ also promised growth in understanding, a guidance "into all the truth." This guidance is given to all the Church, but it has only one authentic definitive voice, that of the bishops speaking in accord with the pope. It takes humility to be guided by these human teachers when one is sure one knows better; so each time the Spirit leads the Church to a fresh statement, we find other lights drifting away. After the First Vatican Council a band of Old Catholics broke away. After Vatican II we find Archbishop Marcel Lefebvre in revolt and theologians openly dissenting from the clear statements of the magisterium. In an understandable gesture of self-defense people turn to fundamentalism, to religion the way it used to be. But fundamentalism is likewise a deafness to the living voice of the Church.

Creationism is a form of biblical fundamentalism, a movement of return to a tradition of finding in Sacred Scripture all that a person needs to know. For creationists this includes the science of nature. For Henry Morris, a creationist leader, "The Bible is a Textbook of Science!" (*Studies in the Bible and Science*, p. 108). Catholics should contrast this with repeated statements of popes since Leo XIII, who, following Saint Augustine, insist that the Bible does *not* teach science.

The view of most Christians, including Catholics, is that God created everything from nothing but did not tell us just how. This view could also be called creationism, since creation is fundamental to it and it rejects all con-

9

trary views of origin, ancient and modern. But the six-day protagonists are known as creationists, so we surrender the title to them.

Creationism stirred up a hornets' nest in this country by attacking the scientific orthodoxy of evolution. This was true of the simply and frankly called biblical creationism of the first half of the century, and it was true again of the scientific creationism of the late 1960s.

To gain perspective on the question we need some history. I am not under the illusion that history can be written without bias. The history presented here will not favor creationism. For that bias the reader is referred to Henry Morris (*A History of Modern Creationism*, 1984).

The history that concerns us is that of views on cosmology (how the world is put together) and cosmogony (how it got that way), as influenced by the Bible. The Bible reflects the cosmogony and cosmology of the ancient Middle East, and in general the Fathers of the Church accepted that, so that it took about a thousand years before Church teachers accepted Greek cosmology, that of Ptolemy.

• Hebrew Cosmology

The Hebrew universe centered on a flat earth, probably rectangular, since the Book of Revelation speaks of the "four corners of the earth" (7:1). It sat on huge pillars. Job speaks of God who "shakes the earth out of its place, and its pillars tremble" (9:6). The Book of Psalms has God himself speaking of this fragile planet we inhabit: "It is I who keep steady its pillars" (75:3). Beneath the center or navel of the earth was cavernous Sheol surrounded by water, which was the source of springs. Above the earth was a great dome, the "firmament" of some translations, a "mirror of cast metal" (Job 37:18, *The Jerusalem Bible*). It "separated the waters which were under the firmament from the waters which were above the firmament" (Genesis 1:7). The windows of the firmament let in the rain and the Deluge (Genesis 7:11). The heavenly bodies moved across the inner surface of this dome.

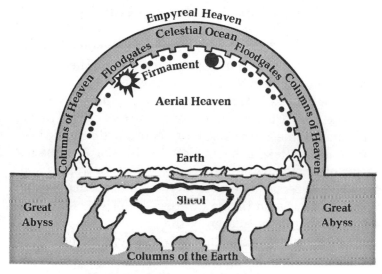

Hebrews' biblical concept of the universe (based on New Catholic Encyclopedia illustration)

• Hebrew Cosmogony

The Hebrew cosmogony is recorded at the beginning of the Book of Genesis, and it is a long stride indeed from that of other Mediterranean peoples. Rejecting the bizarre tales of the emanation of the universe from the bodily members of hominoid gods, the Hebrews tell of a personal God simply creating or calling forth the universe and everything in it by his fiat, his "let it be." Genesis does, how-

11

ever, reflect its folk background in various ways. In particular it tells of creation as a story, with God creating the universe piece by piece like a human workman over a period of time, the period being that of the Mesopotamian workweek of six days. Unlike the day, month, and year, which are marked out by astronomical movements, the week has no natural boundaries and differed in various localities of the ancient world where the dividing day was market day as well as a respite from work. The Hebrews consecrated the Sabbath as a day of worship and rest, and in the creation story God follows the pattern.

The early Church looked for a spiritual as well as a literal sense of the Scriptures. Saint Paul's Letter to the Galatians could be taken as a model (4:22ff). For Paul the narrative of Abraham's two sons born of a slave woman and a free woman becomes an allegory. Hagar is the Jerusalem of the Old Law, Sarah the new Jerusalem of which free children are born, the children of the promise. The Fathers of the Church hardly began to sort out scientific history and cosmology from what they saw as the primary purpose of the Bible, the spiritual nourishment of believers.

Among the Fathers, Saint Augustine gave the closest attention to these questions. After an earlier work on Genesis against the Manicheans, he undertook, between 401 and 405, the writing of twelve books (roughly five hundred pages) entitled *De Genesi ad Literam*, literally "On Genesis to the Letter," or *The Literal Meaning of Genesis*. For Augustine allegorical and figurative meanings were not a problem. He was striving all those years toward an understanding of the literal meaning of especially the first three chapters of Genesis. His advice to his readers was to look first for the meaning intended by the author, using the scriptural context. Failing that, they should choose an interpretation in harmony with the faith (Bk. I, Ch. 21).

12

In cosmology Augustine makes a tentative stab at accommodating the scriptural text and the world view implied in it to the modified Aristotelian physics and astronomy of the fifth century A.D. Thus in Book II, Chapter 1, he asks whether there could be water above the firmament, since water is heavier than air and its proper place is on the earth. He reviews the idea that water as vapor could exist above the air. But his conclusions about cosmology in the Bible remain tentative.

There is nothing tentative, however, about his scorn for those who use their interpretation of the Bible to try to combat secular science. In Book I, Chapter 19, Augustine tells us:

> It often happens that even a non-Christian knows a thing or two about the earth, the sky, the various elements of the world, about the movement and revolution of the stars and even their size and distance, about the anticipated eclipses of the sun and moon, about the nature of animals, shrubs, rocks, and the like, and maintains this knowledge with sure reason and experience. It is then offensive and ruinous, something to be avoided at all cost, for a nonbeliever to hear a Christian talking about these things as though with Christian writings as his source, and yet so nonsensically and with such obvious error that the nonbeliever can hardly keep from laughing.
>
> The trouble is not so much that the erring fellow is laughed at but that our authors are believed by outsiders to have held those same opinions and so are despised and rejected as untutored men, to the great loss of those for whose salvation we toil. . . . How are they going to believe our books concerning the resurrection of the dead, the hope of eternal life, and the kingdom of heaven when they think they are filled

with fallacious writing about things which they know from experience or sure calculation?

There is no telling how much harm these rash and presumptuous people bring upon their more prudent brethren when they begin to be caught and argued down by those who are not bound by the authority of our Scriptures, and when they then try to defend their flippant, rash, and obviously erroneous statements by quoting a shower of words from those same Sacred Scriptures, even citing from memory those passages which they think will support their case, "without understanding either what they are saying or things about which they make assertions" (I Tim. 1:7) [author's translation].

In the next chapter Augustine evens matters somewhat by reproving the other side, the intellectual who belittles Scripture: "Critics full of worldly learning should restrain themselves from attacking as ignorant and uncultured those utterances which have been made to nourish all devout souls. Such critics are like wingless creatures that crawl upon the earth and, while soaring no higher than the leap of a frog, mock the birds in their nests above."

In the Bible the cosmology of the Hebrews, with its flat earth and solid firmament, is implied rather than directly stated. The six days of creation are another matter, and Augustine begins by admitting: "It is a laborious and difficult task for the powers of our human understanding to see clearly the meaning of the sacred writer in the matter of those six days."

For Augustine the problem arose not from scientific evidence for slow evolution but from his theological understanding of the divine operations. We may summarize by saying that while he insisted on God's continuing work of sustaining his creation in existence, as well as on providence and supernatural grace, for the first work of creation he sees no place for a "before and after" on the part of God, for doing one thing one day and another the next. Therefore he prefers to think that everything was created simultaneously, and that those things which did not appear at once were created in their *rationes seminales* (that is, their "root-seeds," or causes), a term that was current among the Stoics. He was aware that the second creation narrative, Genesis 2:4, speaks of the single "day that the LORD made the earth and the heavens," and was not bogged down by the literal six days that bother modern creationists. He was, however, a long way from the modern notion of evolution of species from one another, since he supposed that each "kind" of living thing had been created in its separate "root-seed" (Hessler, p. 12).

• Cosmas Indicopleustes and the Flat-Earth Movement

In the early centuries of the Church, opinion was divided on the shape of the universe. On the one hand the Bible reflected the Mesopotamian view of a flat earth and a vaulted heaven; on the other hand the Greeks thought of the sphere as the ideal shape. Aristotle referred to the curved shadow of the earth on the moon as evidence that the earth is round. Sailors under the clear Mediterranean skies had evidence of the curvature of the earth as the hull of a ship slipped below the horizon before the superstructure.

Eratosthenes (276-194 B.C.) measured this curvature and the size of the earth. Knowing that the sun cast no shadow in Syene (modern Aswan) at noon on the day of the June solstice, whereas at Alexandria it cast a shadow of about seven degrees or one fiftieth of a circle, he calculated

15

the circumference of the earth as fifty times the distance from Alexandria to Syene, which is about five hundred miles to the south. The principle was correct, even though his measurements were rough. Aristarchus of Samos (310-230 B.C.), following the disciples of Pythagoras, anticipated Copernicus by nearly two thousand years with a heliocentric system of planets and fixed stars as we know them; but most Greek thinkers, including the greatest astronomer of antiquity, Hipparchus of Nicea (190-120 B.C.), preferred a system proposed by Eudoxus, a pupil of Plato, of bodies moving in perfect circular motion around a spherical earth. The eccentricities of the planets were explained by epicycles, circular motion around centers some distance from the earth. The system comes down to us in the *Almagest* of Ptolemy (A.D. 85-165). It was the cosmology accepted by the Christian Middle Ages, but since it was a departure from the flat-earth cosmology of the Hebrews, it did not win out without a struggle.

A last-ditch effort in antiquity to vindicate flat-earth cosmology on the basis of Scripture, tradition, and science was made about A.D. 547 in a book called *The Christian Topography* by an Alexandrian, Cosmas Indicopleustes, a world traveler turned monk. On page 4 we read: "Some supposed to be Christian, holding divine scripture of no account but despising the looking down upon it, assume like the pagan philosophers that the form of the heavens is spherical, being led into this error by the solar and lunar eclipses."

In a rambling argument Cosmas cites the scriptural evidence that the sacred writers thought the earth was flat and surmounted by a firmament. He also enlists the opinions of some of the Fathers, notably Saint John Chrysostom, who says, "Where are those who say the heaven is in motion? Where are those who think it is

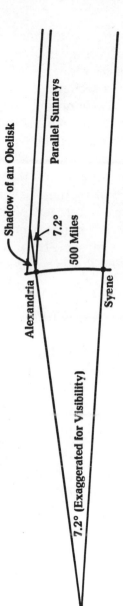

Shadow of an Obelisk

Parallel Sunrays

Alexandria

7.2°

500 Miles

Syene

7.2° (Exaggerated for Visibility)

Eratosthenes's measurement of the earth's circumference

spherical? For both these opinions are here swept away" (p. 347), namely by the passage in Hebrews (8:2) which refers to the heavenly sanctuary.

Cosmas's world is a rectangular box, like the Ark of the Covenant, with a flat floor and a flat firmament supported by walls which are longer on the north and south sides. There is a vaulted chamber above the flat firmament. The sun, moon, and stars move across the heavens by angel power. "The luminaries of the heavens are not moved by the revolution of the heavens, but rather by powers that are rational, as if they were so many torch-bearers. . . . Some of the angels were commissioned to move the air, some the sun, some the moon, some the stars, while others prepared the clouds and the rains" (p. 76).

Cosmas props up his objections to Greek astronomical theory by arguments which could be called a fledgling flat-earth science. On a spherical earth, he says, people on the antipodes, "down under," would have their heads downward, and rivers would flow backward (p. 17). If the earth were a sphere, there would be parts on which the sun does not shine (p. 262). With a stab at scientific method he drove a nail into a globe and found that the shadow was round, not conical, so the sun could not be very large (p. 259).

Cosmas's efforts were not universally acclaimed even in antiquity. In the ninth century, Photius, patriarch of Constantinople, writes: "He makes up stories so incredible that he may fairly be regarded as a writer of fables rather than of facts" (p. iii). A later writer cites his work "as a memorable example of that mischievous process of loading Christian truth with the dead weight of false science" (p. xxi).

From our vantage point Cosmas shows great sincerity in his zeal to preserve biblical revelation from the contamination of pagan science but little else. He overshoots

18

the mark through the fundamentalist error of making the Bible say something it does not say. The Bible does not teach that the earth was flat; it only reflects the common assumption of the people of the Middle East that it was flat. He undershoots the mark with his science. For the inhabitants of the antipodes, as we are to the Australians, "down" is where gravity draws us. He confuses the apparent size of the sun, which depends on its distance, with its actual size. His nail, as anyone can show on a sunny day, casts a sharp shadow when close to the receiving surface, a more diffuse one as it is moved farther away. The conical shape of the full shadow in the center is obscured by the diffuse penumbra. And so Cosmas falls squarely under Saint Augustine's censure of those who invite ridicule of the Bible by using it badly against contemporary science.

If refuting Cosmas looks like beating a dead horse, please be patient! The purpose is to show that the methods of modern creation scientists are not new, and while they are more sophisticated, they are really not much better than the old.

• The Modern Flat-Earth Movement

Between the effort of Cosmas in the sixth century and the medieval revival of learning, the spherical astronomy of Ptolemy gradually became the common view of educated people, in India and the Moslem world as well as in Europe; it was a clear case of the defeat of a fundamentalist biblical interpretation. The seemingly more biblical flat-earth cosmology gave way to "pagan science." Incidentally it is naïve to say, as elementary textbooks used to do, that the people of Columbus's time thought he would sail off the edge of the earth. Those who thought so were as ignorant in their time as the writers of those textbooks were in ours.

Flat-earthism, though out of step with current thought

since antiquity, has not died out completely. The modern movement began in 1865 when there appeared in London a book called *Zetetic Astronomy, Earth Not a Globe! An Experimental Inquiry into the True Figure of the Earth: Proving It a Plane, Without Axial or Orbital Motion; and the Only Material World in the Universe*. Its author was "Parallax," a pen name for Samuel Rowbotham. Like Cosmas, he wants to safeguard faith in the Bible, although he mutes his intention until the latter part of the book. He espouses a "zetetic" method, which eschews hypothesis and just puts the facts on the table. ("Zetetic" comes from the Greek *zētein*, to seek for, to investigate.)

The universe he puts together is no longer shaped like the Ark of the Covenant but like a disk, the center of which is the North Pole, since following the polestar always leads there. The outer circumference is the South "Pole," a great ring of ice. The heavenly bodies move across the sky from east to west and disappear behind the circumference to go around to the east side once more.

As might be expected, most of the book is devoted to rebuttal or to alternate explanations of the observations that seem to point to a spherical earth. His best effort goes into counteracting the Greek observation that ships disappearing over the horizon sink out of sight bottom first instead of just diminishing to nothing in the distance. Do they really disappear hull first? No, says Parallax.

To prove that they do not, he sought out a calm and straight stretch of water and found it in the Old Bedford Canal in Cambridge County, twenty miles without a bend. Here, claimed Parallax, one should be able to see the curvature of the earth if it exists, since according to a railroad formula, an object some miles away should drop below the level of the viewing point by eight inches times the square of the distance in miles from the object.

This is how Parallax describes the experiment, which turned out to his entire satisfaction: "A boat with a flag standing 3 feet above the water was directed to sail from a place called 'Welney Bridge' to another place called 'Welche's Dam.' These two points are six statute miles apart. The observer, with a good telescope, was seated in the water as a bather (it being the summer season) with the eye not exceeding eight inches above the surface. The flag and the boat down to the water's edge were clearly visible throughout the whole distance! From this observation it was concluded that the water did not decline to any degree from the line of sight; whereas the water would be 6 feet higher in the center of an arc of 6 miles extent than at the two places Welney Bridge and Welche's Dam; but as the eye of the observer was only eight inches above the water, the highest point of the surface would be at one mile from the place of observation, below which point the surface of the water at the end of the remaining five miles would be 11 feet 8 inches (5^2x8 = 200 inches)" (p. 11).

Parallax mentions a number of locations, such as lighthouses and promontories, from which the curvature of the earth should be observable but is not. He says that the hull of a ship seems to disappear first because it is smaller than the sails. A good telescope will bring the hull back into sight. Then as if mistrusting that eventuality, he revises the laws of perspective. If you sight along a long row of lampposts, he says, at the level of the top of the pedestal, the pedestal will vanish to a point before the lamps, which are farther from the level of the eye, because "parallel lines converge at the same point only if they are equidistant from the eye line." *(See illustration on next page.)*

To the argument that Magellan circumnavigated the globe Parallax of course responds that he circumnavigated the disk. No one had ever sailed around the South Pole.

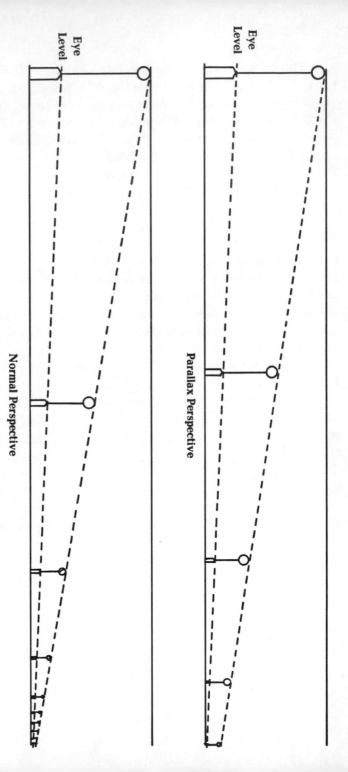

Graphs showing the Parallax perspective as opposed to normal perspective

Lieutenant (later Rear Admiral) Charles Wilkes of the United States Navy tried but failed. To the argument that the sun seems to rise out of the earth he replies that its closeness to the earth is an optical effect of distance. To the objection that the same distance which makes the sun seem to touch the earth should reduce its apparent size to a point he replies that the atmosphere acts as a lens to enlarge the apparent size.

An interesting sequel to the appearance of Parallax's book is found in the news of 1870. An ardent flat-earthist, John Hampden, bet five hundred pounds that no one could prove the curvature of the earth by observation across a body of water, and the bet was taken by Alfred Russel Wallace, the famous evolutionist. On the same Old Bedford Canal, flags were placed on two bridges six miles apart and a third one on a post halfway between, all thirteen feet above water. When the telescope was leveled at the first bridge, the other two flags dropped below the crosshair by the amount expected on a sphere of four thousand miles radius, according to Mr. Curtis, who was Mr. Wallace's observer and second. Mr. Carpenter, who was Mr. Hampden's observer and second, and who, it turned out, had himself written a book promoting a flat earth, disagreed. The impasse was overcome when the holder of the stakes came out for a second look and declared Wallace the winner. Hampden pursued Wallace for years with scurrilous tracts and lawsuits, and although Hampden spent time in jail for libel and never got the prize money, Wallace could boast of no more than a Pyrrhic victory (Schadewald, see bibliography).

With regard to Parallax's science, we may observe that the experience of looking at a flag six miles away through a telescope may be shaky enough to allow room for wishful thinking. Another choice is to view a beachline across a wide lake from a vantage point of varying height. This makes objects on the opposite shore appear and disappear. Since California's flat-earthists were unable to observe this effect across Lake Tahoe or the Salton Sea, they are invited to Grand Lake in Ohio, where it is quite clear! Also when a freighter on Lake Michigan is viewed from various heights on the dunes of the southern shore, parts of the ship disappear in a very convincing way. The Greeks saw this, but a telescope is a great help.

Concerning the laws of perspective that Parallax proposes, note that parallel lines in Euclidean geometry do not converge to a point except at infinity, which in the real world is never, and that they maintain the same relative distance from one another as far as they go.

One might suppose that with the world travel and empire building of the nineteenth century to confirm Copernican and Newtonian astronomy, the flat-earthists would finally throw in the towel, but the stakes are too high for the fundamentalists. In the opinion of Parallax Newtonian astronomy "is a prolific source of irreligion and of atheism, of which its advocates are, practically, supporters. . . . [Because of] the differences between the language of Scripture and the teachings of modern Astronomy, there is to be found in the very hearts of Christian and Jewish congregations a sort of smouldering scepticism . . . which has led thousands to desert the cause of earnest, active Christianity, and which has forced the majority of those who remain in the ranks of religion to declare that the Scriptures were not intended to teach correctly other than moral and religious doctrines, that the references so often made to the physical world, and to material phenomena generally, are given in a language to suit the prevailing notions and ignorance of the people" (p. 184).

There has been some development in the majority in-

24

terpretation of Scripture which he cites already in 1865, and which he deplores, but the fundamentalist battle lines were already drawn. The Flat Earth Society, Schadewald tells us, moved from England to Zion, Illinois, and then to Lancaster, California, becoming a neighbor to Edwards Air Force Base, the home of the space shuttle, where it must contend, not with the shadow of the earth on the moon, but with color photographs of a spheroid earth, complete with clouds, oceans, and continents. The Society's president, Charles Johnson, is not daunted. For him the whole space program is faked, a carnival put on Hollywood-style to fool the people into accepting the spheroid-earth hypothesis of the scientists. The Society's publications, which reprint the arguments of Parallax, are available to members, who must be true believers and who number about six hundred.

* Early Evolutionism

We have seen that there are still biblical fundamentalists who insist on a flat earth seventeen centuries after Ptolemy, in this age of moon travel and space exploration. There are also geocentrists who five hundred years after Copernicus (Godfrey, p. 295) believe that the sun goes around the earth because the Book of Joshua (10:12-14), quoting a "Book of the Jashar," speaks of the sun as standing still in the middle of the sky and delaying its setting for almost a whole day. And there are fundamentalists who a century after Darwin maintain that each living species was created separately in its present form in a six-day creation six thousand years ago. The three groups are fired with the same zeal for preserving an unofficial and minority interpretation of the Bible against established scientific opinion, even though they do not work together.

Creationism as a fighting word developed slowly over the centuries, because the evidence against it was discov-

25

ered slowly. Gradually signs of volcanism, mineralization, sedimentation, and fossilization were observed by such notables as Saint Albert in the thirteenth century, Agricola in the fifteenth, and Ray in the seventeenth, leading to the acceptance of a dynamic, changing earth. The first theory proposed to account for these changes within a span of six thousand years was catastrophism. Thomas Burnet offered a Deluge catastrophe theory in 1681, and in 1696 Whiston, with Newton's approval, proposed in his *New Theory of the Earth* that a passing comet may have caused the Great Flood by tipping the axis of the earth (Patten, p. 32). Modern creationists in general espouse analogous catastrophe theories.

The six-thousand-year calendar was abandoned by Georges Buffon (1707-1788) in his *Histoire Naturelle*, which was published over a fifty-year period. It was further upset by the Scotsman James Hutton in his *Theory of the Earth* of 1788. Hutton's theory was that the processes observable in the present — such as igneous intrusion, volcanism, erosion by water and wind, and sedimentation — had gone on long enough to produce the present features of the earth, including the sea sediments on what are now the tops of mountains. This is the principle of uniformitarianism, which is the bane of modern creationists, since obviously a few thousand years will never do for such processes. Uniformitarianism was strongly supported after Charles Lyell's *Principles of Geology* came out in 1830-1833. Modern methodological uniformitarianism means that nature's laws are constant, not that every process goes on forever at the same speed (Young, p. 143).

The development of life-forms had been stressed by Buffon, and in 1784 Erasmus Darwin in *Zoonomia* proposed the full-fledged evolutionary theory that new species arose by natural selection, as his grandson Charles was to do

26

more effectively two generations later. In 1809 Jean Baptiste de Lamarck came out with his *Philosophie Zoologique*, in which he proposed a different mechanism for evolution, namely, the inheritance of acquired characteristics. For example, a giraffe stretches its neck to reach higher branches for succulent leaves and as a result its offspring inherit longer necks. The theory has been repeatedly discredited and buried only to rise again. Robert Chambers, cofounder of the *Chambers Encyclopedia*, came out in 1844 with *Vestiges of the Natural History of Creation*, a thoroughgoing evolutionary work which, following Laplace's nebular hypothesis, proposed that the world started on its way as a cloud of dust.

An attempt to stem this evolutionary tide was made in 1857 by Philip Gosse, a British naturalist and biblical fundamentalist, in his book *Omphalos* (the Greek word for navel), and the book became famous for claiming that fossils were created as they are now found in such a way as to suggest a long history of the earth even though it was only about six thousand years old. In this, said Gosse, there was no more deception on the part of the Creator than there was in endowing Adam with a navel, a sign that he had a natural parent when he really had none. This surely brought the problem of excessive literalism out into the open, and it is not surprising that the book failed to fulfill the author's aim of shoring up the fundamentalist interpretation of Genesis.

The stage was thus set for the entry of Charles Darwin, who stole the show not because he discovered evolution or settled its problems but because he and those who agreed with him argued their case well at the right time. Two decades after the voyage of the *Beagle*, spurred on by reading a preliminary draft of what Alfred Russel Wallace was planning to publish on the same topic, Darwin

27

gathered his copious notes and preliminary sketches and published *On the Origin of Species by Means of Natural Selection or the Preservation of Favored Races in the Struggle for Life*. The casual reader may find heavy going through the plethora of examples, but in 1859 the book was an immediate success, and it has since proved to be the most influential scientific treatise since Newton's *Principia*. Darwin deliberately avoided discussing human evolution at the time, waiting until 1871, when his reputation was more solidly established, before coming out with *The Descent of Man and Selection in Relation to Sex*.

Readers of James Moore's *The Post-Darwinian Controversies* or Boller's *American Thought in Transition* will discover that most of the good ideas in the debate between creationists and evolutionists had already been hammered out before the turn of the century. Many scientists who encountered Darwinism in their prime, such as Charles Lyell and Louis Agassiz, were as disturbed by the notion of evolution of species as were the general run of divines. The noted German pathologist Rudolf Virchow, though favoring transformism (that is, evolution), voted against teaching Darwinism in German schools (Clark, p. 214). On the other hand, as James Moore tells us in his book (pp. 263-264), the Anglican minister Aubrey Lackington Moore reached this conclusion:

> If the theory of special creation existed in the Bible or in Christian antiquity, we might bravely try and do battle for it. But it came to us some two centuries ago from the side of science, with the imprimatur of a Puritan poet [Milton]. . . .
>
> Cataclysmic geology and special creation are the scientific analogue of Deism. Order, development, law, are the analogue of the Christian view of God.

A very revealing confession that creationism is a fairly new doctrine comes from Henry Morris himself. He tells us: "For almost 300 years, following the Reformation, the hoary pagan philosophies of evolution and the eternity of matter had been rejected, and pure Biblical creationism was believed and taught almost everywhere. But, as soon as the scientists turned to evolution, theologians and church leaders in almost every denomination scurried in a hasty retreat to the old compromising types of exegesis used by early theologians, such as Origen and Augustine, in order to accommodate evolution and the geological ages in Genesis" (1984, p. 37).

• Twentieth-Century Anti-Evolutionism

Fundamentalist opposition to evolution crystallized in a number of organizations devoted to defending the Bible against the spirit of the age, the most influential being the World's Christian Fundamental Association founded in 1918. Within a few years after the first World War the fundamentalist tide had brought about the passage of laws against the teaching of evolution in public schools in Oklahoma, Florida, and Mississippi, while similar laws failed to pass in other states.

Early in 1925 the Tennessee law against teaching evolution was signed by the governor and quickly brought on the sideshow of the century in the courtroom of the county seat of Dayton. John Scopes, a young coach and science teacher there, agreed to challenge the law. He was abetted by the American Civil Liberties Union from New York and defended by Clarence Darrow. The prosecutor was William Jennings Bryan, who won the case, such as it was. Expert witnesses were barred from testifying, and Scopes had already confessed, even though he admitted later that he missed class the day he was supposed to talk about evolution and so never broke the law.

29

Both sides could be declared losers in the case. While the law remained on the Tennessee books until 1967, the other states contemplating such laws quickly backed off and creationism was denied the legal avenue. Furthermore the press made the fundamentalists look like monkeys on the evolutionary tree. On the other hand, while evolution had a free hand legally, schools now handled it with asbestos gloves, if at all, so that evolutionist Stephen Jay Gould complains (p. 283) that the text from which he studied biology in high school in 1956, by Moon, Mason, and Otto, treated evolution in "one pussyfooting chapter" without even mentioning the word.

The situation changed in the very next year, 1957, when Sputnik rose into orbit and American schools were caught short with their cafeteria education system. The immediate call was for more engineers, but the National Science Foundation also liberally funded the Biological Sciences Curriculum Study of 1959, which resulted in new high-school biology textbooks based on evolution as the "warp and woof of modern biology." These texts were eventually used by half the students in the country and other texts followed their lead.

The fundamentalists were ready. During the relatively calm years from 1925 to 1957 the creationist groups brought out anti-evolution literature in England and the United States. In 1935 the Religion and Science Association was formed in America. Next came the Creation-Deluge Society which lasted from 1938 to 1945 and consisted mostly of Seventh-Day Adventists, who were early champions of the cause. The American Scientific Affiliation was organized in 1941. While members of these associations were committed to a literal interpretation of Genesis and opposed Darwinism, they embraced a wide spectrum of views on geological dating, the Deluge, and other matters, so that

30

splinter groups were inevitable (Morris, 1984). Over a period of years Dr. Henry Morris of Virginia Polytechnic Institute, collaborating with Dr. John Whitcomb of Grace Theological Seminary in Winona, Indiana, worked out the intensively researched and seminal creationist book *The Genesis Flood,* which was first published in 1961.

After the triumphal centennial celebration of Darwin's *Origin of Species* in 1959 and the successful insertion of evolution into high-school texts, a number of creationist and anti-evolutionist associations arose. Of these the most prominent has been the Creation Research Society formed in Asbury, Kentucky, and Midland, Michigan, in 1963 and now numbering some six hundred members. The title reflects the realization that the battle is for the minds of students, especially in high school, and that laws forbidding the teaching of evolution in public schools had little chance of surviving the constitutional challenge. The new strategy is to engage trained scientists — all members must have advanced degrees in natural science — to undertake in-depth research to prove that the evidence of nature favors a short history of the universe and that a single cataclysmic flood accounts for geological features better than continental drift and continuous uniformitarian processes.

New laws were introduced into a number of states which would require that this creation science be taught, if not instead of evolution, at least as an alternate explanation, so that the students would be able to choose for themselves, Deweyan fashion, concerning this most fundamental question of the origin of things. They would of course be swayed by the most skillful rhetoric, and there were numerous debates in these decades, usually on college campuses, which the creationists won handily until a few evolutionists took them seriously. In 1977 an Indiana judge ruled that the creationist text *Biology: A Search for Order*

31

in Complexity could not be used in Indiana public schools.

The best-publicized two-model law was that of Arkansas, enacted in March 1981, challenged in May of the same year by the American Civil Liberties Union, tried with all the publicity if not the ballyhoo of the Scopes trial of 1925, and struck down by Judge William Overton's decision of January 1982. Representatives of the major religious groups, including Catholic, signed as plaintiffs in the suit against the law requiring creationist science in schools. Their concern was the preservation of the religious liberty guaranteed by the Constitution against the establishment by law of a particular interpretation of the Bible thinly disguised as science. A similar law was struck down in Louisiana in January 1985 and the appeal refused in July 1985.

Judge Overton spoke for a wide segment of the population when he wrote: "The theory of evolution assumes the existence of life and is directed to an explanation of how life evolved. Evolution does not presuppose the absence of a creator or God. . . . The idea that belief in a creator and acceptance of the scientific theory of evolution are mutually exclusive is a false premise and offensive to the religious views of many" (Frye, p. 77).

2

Critique of Creation Science

Catholic reviewers are sometimes favorably impressed by the scientific arguments of the creationists, and Catholic fundamentalists claim that evolutionists have no answer for them. For a critique by scientists the reader is referred to *Scientists Confront Creationism*, a collection of essays edited by Laurie Godfrey, and for the religious viewpoint to *Christianity and the Age of the Earth*, by Davis Young, and *Is God a Creationist?* edited by Roland Frye. Here I shall address the one question that seems crucial to their case: Can they get beyond a negative criticism of evolution and give positive reasons for thinking that the earth and the universe are young?

First, we must try to summarize what they teach. Twentieth-century creationists go along with twentieth-century cosmology for the most part, abandoning the flat-earthists and geocentrists to their own devices. They have fallen back to the last bastion of Bible-derived science, six-day creation cosmogony. Their doctrine ought to be simple: God created the various parts of the universe, including each living species, in essentially their present state some six thousand years ago. But confronted by modern evolutionary cosmogonies, creationism has become complex, varied, and even elusive. We may say that it has evolved to fit the newer science. In it creation and the Deluge are closely joined and complementary in a way that could hardly have crossed the minds of the Hebrew writers of Genesis.

The creationist story goes something like this. At some time in the past, thousands rather than millions or billions of years ago, God created the universe in its present form in the order given in the first chapter of Genesis. Stars and galaxies were created at distances of millions or billions of light-years from the earth and from one another, but this does not mean that all that time actually elapsed. When God said "Let there be light," light was created throughout the universe at vast distances from what seems to us to be its source, the stars. Likewise the stars were created in various stages of maturity, and the nuclear processes now assumed to be taking place in them were not actually their birth and death processes. Stars have only the appearance of great age. In the words of Henry Morris: "At some point in time . . . the Space/Mass/Time cosmos was simply created, brought into existence, in fully developed and functioning form right from the beginning. The complex structures of its immense variety of stars and galaxies did not evolve at all. They were simply created, with any changes since that time limited to processes of decay, not development" (1982, p. 228).

Changes in the earth since its creation have been rather drastic. According to the creationist model the earth was originally fitted out with a very considerable canopy of water vapor in the upper atmosphere, the biblical "firmament." (The possibility, as noted earlier, was considered by Saint Augustine.) Such a canopy would have some interesting properties. Since it would be as transparent as air to visible radiation but would absorb and reflect the infrared, it would bring about a large greenhouse effect that would tend to keep the world climate mild and even tropical right up to the polar regions. It would also absorb ultraviolet radiation, which is supposed to be responsible for much of the aging process (Morris, 1972, p. 29). Protected from this destructive radiation the patriarchs could live a thousand years as readily as we live a hundred.

Then came the Deluge. "The Flood itself appears to have been due to a combination of meteorological and tectonic phenomena. The 'fountains of the deep' emitted great quantities of juvenile water and magmatic materials, and the 'waters above the firmament,' probably an extensive thermal atmospheric blanket of water vapor, condensed and precipitated torrential rains for a period of forty days" (Morris, 1969, p. 328).

Although creationists do not embrace Velikovsky as a kindred spirit, they do envision a worldwide catastrophe reminiscent of his *Worlds in Collision*, caused perhaps by a near brush with another planet whose gravitational field set the earth's outer layers flopping like a jelly, not only triggering the rapid condensation of the vapor canopy to give the world its first rainfall but also releasing magma and rock-bound water from the crust (Patten, p. 66).

35

This "deluge" profoundly altered the earth's surface, raising the mountains, confining the oceans to smaller and deeper troughs, and leaving behind mile-thick deposits such as those observed in the Grand Canyon or on mountains of sedimentary rock, which geologists usually ascribe to slow deposition and orogeny (mountain-making) lasting millions of years. The fossils of the animals that perished appear in logical order, the larger specimens and stronger swimmers above the smaller ones, since they survived longer, giving evolutionists the impression that the larger ones existed at a later period than the smaller and evolved from them. Sea life also, which would not drown in any amount of water, was overwhelmed by the earth movement and so appears in fossil form. Coal beds and petroleum deposits could easily have formed in the year of the Great Flood, or they could have been created in their present condition.

From this catastrophe air-breathing species were saved in the Ark in pairs, seven pairs each in the case of the "clean" animals. Zoologists number species in the millions, but creationists are satisfied with the biblical "kinds" (baramin, from the Hebrew for "created kind"), fewer in number, which could have contained the present varieties in their genetic code. Most species are insects, which do not take up much room, so the Ark described in the Bible was probably adequate (Filby, p. 100). Taking the cubit as eighteen inches makes the Ark 450 feet long, 75 feet wide, and 45 feet high, surely the largest vessel of ancient times. There was room for all species of animals, together with a year's supply of food, though perhaps some animals went into hibernation. The earlier and more frankly biblical creationists had more leeway for miraculous intervention in these matters than the later creation scientists. The model assumes that species which have been uncovered as fossil remains and are now extinct, such as dinosaurs and mastodons, somehow missed the boat or became extinct after the Flood. Dinosaurs, for example, could have been on board in the form of eggs.

We may observe parenthetically here that the vapor canopy providing the "waters above the firmament" could not have contributed much to this worldwide flood. A vapor canopy with enough water to cover Mount Ararat at 17,000 feet would have the same mass as that same water in liquid form and would exert a vapor pressure at sea level equal to that of a column of water 17,000 feet, or 5,000 meters, in depth, namely 500 kilograms per square centimeter. That is 500 times our atmospheric pressure. Since the critical pressure of water is only 220 atmospheres, this 500-atmosphere water would have to be at a temperature near our boiling point of water to remain a vapor, and would have a density about one third that of liquid water. These would have been incredible living conditions for Noah and his ancestors. Even if atmospheric vapor had added only thirty feet to the Flood, atmospheric pressure would have been reduced to one half its previous value.

The water supply for the Flood might have been orbiting the earth after capture from an ice comet (cf. Morris, in *Stonehenge Viewpoint*, May-June 1985) and so escaped the force of gravity which would produce the enormous pressure. And of course if the mountains were raised to their present height by the "deluge," perhaps not so much water was needed.

• The Young-Universe Arguments

To promote their scheme from fantasy to plausibility, all the creationists need to do is demonstrate that the world is only a few thousand years old. According to creationist Thomas G. Barnes (*Christianity Today*, October 8, 1982,

p. 28), "it takes only one proof of a young age to refute completely the evolutionary hypothesis." Conversely of course it takes only one proof of even a million-year existence of the earth to destroy completely the hypothesis of six-day creationism. Henry Morris (1977, pp. 58ff) lists seventy arguments for a young earth. In the interest of brevity I shall use the thirty-three of Wysong (pp. 159-178), which cover the same ground, and gather them under five headings. Catholic fundamentalists insist that we take them seriously, so let us imagine ourselves attending one of the many debates which the creationists won so handily over more than a decade, listening to these arguments. We may have experience in some science (chemistry teaching in my case) but need consultation in others. We are busy taking notes and imagining how we might balance the arguments with a response from the evolutionist side.

A. Biohistory

QUESTION AT ISSUE: If man has been here for millions of years, why do we only find records of man dating to about 3000 B.C.?

RESPONSE: Written history goes back only five thousand years because writing was a late invention. Other artifacts, especially works of art, are much more ancient and just as characteristic of human genius.

QUESTION AT ISSUE: At a modest population growth rate one couple would have generated the present four billion people in only a few thousand years (cf. Williams, p. 4).

RESPONSE: Wysong uses an impressive mathematical formula which really amounts to a 50 percent increase per generation, giving a total population of 1.5^n where n is the number of generations. He uses 1,820 years, or 52 generations, to arrive at a population of 4.34 billion. A creationist, however, should use 6,000 years, or 180 gener-

38

ations, which would give a total of 10^{32} for the present population. For comparison, the mass of the earth is 6×10^{28} grams. We conclude that naïve extrapolation tells us nothing about the age of the human race.

QUESTION AT ISSUE: The oldest living things, the bristlecone pines, which conceivably could live much longer, are only about six thousand years old, the biblical age of the earth.

RESPONSE: Most living things die in a much shorter time. There is no conceivable connection here with the age of the earth.

QUESTION AT ISSUE: It is agreed that most mutations are harmful. The present mutation rate extended over millions of years would have piled up an intolerable "mutation load" in modern biota.

RESPONSE: Evolutionary theory has harmful mutations filtered out by natural selection, but it is not a settled issue. We note that this argument, like many of the thirty-three, is not direct evidence for a young earth but a possible difficulty arising from an old one.

B. The Atmosphere

QUESTION AT ISSUE: Vegetation would produce the present oxygen level in about five thousand years.

RESPONSE: The oxygen level of the atmosphere is at a fairly stable equilibrium. Oxygen is formed by photosynthesis at the same rate as it is used up by oxidation processes which speed up when the oxygen concentration rises. Most of these processes supply the carbon dioxide needed for photosynthesis. This equilibrium could have been reached billions of years ago. It is poor creationist strategy to argue that the earth was created with zero atmospheric oxygen.

QUESTION AT ISSUE: Radioactivity would have produced

the present level of atmospheric helium in ten thousand years.

RESPONSE: It is generally held that the light gases, hydrogen and helium, escape rather quickly from the earth's gravitational field, so the present level of these gases would have no bearing on the age of the earth.

QUESTION AT ISSUE: Carbon-14, or C-14, formation rate exceeds the decay rate by a ratio of twenty-seven to sixteen, so that the present level of C-14 should have been reached in eight thousand years. Very long periods should have brought about dynamic equilibrium, the rates becoming equal.

RESPONSE: C-14 is formed when atmospheric nitrogen-14 captures a neutron from secondary cosmic rays and gives off a proton. Cosmic rays fluctuate with solar flares. The fluctuation is buffered by the Van Allen belts, which shield the lower atmosphere, but we still expect some oscillation around the equilibrium value.

QUESTION AT ISSUE: The quantity of inert gas found adsorbed on lunar dust would accumulate in a few thousand years from its source in the "solar wind."

RESPONSE: The special issue of *Science* of January 30, 1970, reports the results of careful analyses of lunar samples in various laboratories of the world after the 1969 landing. The author cited by Wysong hardly supports him. He concludes: "A few hundred million years are needed to obtain the observed helium loading of the ilmenite surface down to a depth of about 60 cm." The understanding is that the inert gases carried on the "solar wind" are adsorbed on the fine dust of the lunar surface, the heavier elements below argon gradually displacing the more volatile and less adhesive helium in the surface layers. The fact that gases are found at a depth of sixty centimeters suggests some plowing of the land by meteorites.

40

It is interesting to speculate whether scientists would have bothered with these painstaking measurements without the theory of evolution to spur them to a deeper understanding of the history of the solar system.

C. Geology

QUESTION AT ISSUE: The present level of topsoil would accumulate in a few thousand years.

RESPONSE: And just as easily wash away and be renewed over millions of years.

QUESTION AT ISSUE: On the other hand, erosion over millions of years should have worn everything smooth and made the river deltas much larger than they are.

RESPONSE: This line of talk completely ignores plate tectonics, continental drift, orogeny, and degradation-aggradation that take place at an observable pace before our eyes.

QUESTION AT ISSUE: Long erosion should have produced a much different mix of minerals dissolved or suspended in the oceans.

RESPONSE: The evidence Wysong cites for a brief lifespan of the oceans because of the proportions of the elements found in them is actually a chart of estimates of the time it would take for each element to reach its present concentration at the addition rates estimated for the present. They range from eighty years for cerium to two hundred sixty million years for sodium. Wysong then concludes: "Vast age or short age can be argued with equal scientific uniformitarian ease." In other words, the chart tells us nothing about the age of the oceans. We agree.

QUESTION AT ISSUE: Ocean bottoms show too little ooze from decaying biota to fit the evolutionary time span.

RESPONSE: Organic matter is recycled through the biota of the oceans. Then we note that the ocean basins have not

41

always been ocean basins. Continental drift has altered the sea bottoms. Furthermore many foraminiferal oozes are found as foraminiferal limestones, deposited from shallow seas where sea life is at its most intense. (Foraminifera is an order of sea animals with shells.)

QUESTION AT ISSUE: The Niagara Gorge was cut by the Falls in a few thousand years.

RESPONSE: Niagara Falls and the Great Lakes date from the latest ice age, not from the beginning of the world.

QUESTION AT ISSUE: If strata like those exposed in the Grand Canyon "were built up gradually, each layer would have been eroded to a more or less degree obliterating any horizontal continuity. Therefore the creationist insists that the horizontal plates of strata must have been deposited rapidly."

RESPONSE: Creationists make a great effort to explain the Grand Canyon, as well they might. High-school students tend to snicker when told that the biblical Flood deposited it all in one year.

As proposed already by Nicholas Steno in the seventeenth century, marine deposition produces lateral continuity in the strata. Continental deposition varies from horizontal to cross-bedding. Except at the mouth of a stream, erosion takes place on land, not in the sea, so there is no reason to think the horizontal continuity should be obliterated.

The common, almost self-evident interpretation of the Grand Canyon is that the Colorado River sliced down through a mile of sedimentary deposits right into the igneous rocks below during a period of continental uplift. That took time.

QUESTION AT ISSUE: Stalactites have been observed to form rapidly. In one case in Carlsbad Caverns a bat was encased in the onyx before it had time to decompose.

42

RESPONSE: Stalactites and stalagmites in limestone caves come and go rather rapidly on the geological time scale. They do not date the beginning of the world.

QUESTION AT ISSUE: The present rate of volcanic activity should have produced much more water and volcanic rock over billions of years than we actually find.

RESPONSE: Wysong cites *The Genesis Flood* of Henry Morris, who gives a figure of three hundred forty million years as a maximum age of the earth based on the quantity of water in the ocean. Remember that they are trying to prove scientifically that the earth is only six thousand years old. Also much of the volcanic water is recycled vadose and ground water.

QUESTION AT ISSUE: Extrapolating backward from the present decay rate of the earth's magnetic field allows an age of only about ten thousand years before the energy level of the magnetic field becomes intolerably high.

RESPONSE: There is no scientific reason for supposing a steady decrease in the earth's magnetic field. Creationists abominate uniformitarianism unless they can invoke it to fit their theory. At one level magnetic theory is beautifully simple: where electrical charges move relative to each other there is a magnetic field at right angles to the motion. But the application to the earth's magnetic field is a composite of educated guesses.

One piece of evidence is enough to destroy the creationist case (Godfrey, pp. 36, 76). The Atlantic Ocean is spreading measurably at the central ridge. As the magma intrudes, it is magnetized by the earth's field when hot, and remains magnetized when it cools below the Curie point. Cores taken from this ridge show that the earth's magnetic field has reversed itself repeatedly, at intervals of roughly half a million years, over the past two hundred million years.

QUESTION AT ISSUE: At the high pressure existing in petroleum deposits the oil should have bled off into the surrounding rocks in a few thousand years.

RESPONSE: At times oil does seep to the surface to form tar pits, but most of it stays put, since there are no regions of lower pressure available. The article cited by Wysong merely reports a study of hydrostatic pressure that builds up in water trapped during the process of faulting, when of course shifts can be expected.

D. Cosmic Dust

QUESTION AT ISSUE: (1) Cosmic dust should have covered the earth to a depth of fifty feet in several billion years. (2) If the cosmic dust washed into the oceans, the oceans should show a higher nickel content than the earth's crust.

RESPONSE: Some meteorites are indeed richer in nickel and cobalt than the earth's crust, leading scientists to conclude that the core of the earth is also richer in these metals than is the crust. Iron forms the lighter oxides more readily than nickel or cobalt, so on the hypothesis that the earth formed by the accumulation of cosmic material we would expect the heavier cobalt and nickel compounds to sink deeper.

Wysong's argument might carry more weight but for the fact that Hans Petterson, the author he cites and the researcher in the case, finds that the nickel in the seabeds matches the estimate of meteorite fall (*Scientific American*, February 1960, p. 123).

QUESTION AT ISSUE: The large observable meteoric craters all seem to have been formed in the past few thousand years.

RESPONSE: Petterson agrees that "even larger meteorites become lost in the turnover of material of the earth's surface; there are no 'fossil' materials, that is, none more than

44

25,000 years old." This does not mean that all meteorites fell in the past twenty-five thousand years, or six thousand years.

E. Astronomy

QUESTION AT ISSUE: "The lunar surface is exposed to direct sunlight, and strong ultra-violet light and X-rays can destroy the surface layers of exposed rock and reduce them to dust" at a rate which would make the dust twenty to sixty miles thick if the moon is five or ten billion years old. The first men on the moon found only a thin layer of dust.

RESPONSE: Highly energetic radiation does indeed change the molecules it encounters. In the earth's upper atmosphere it ionizes oxygen and nitrogen, produces and destroys ozone, sprays out secondary cosmic rays. But the same upper layer of gases undergoes the same reactions repeatedly, using up the energy so that only a small part of the radiation reaches the earth. On the lunar surface also the radiation should constantly remodel the crystal structures, leaving a powder, but the same surface powder would keep absorbing the radiation so that it could reach a depth of only a few centimeters.

QUESTION AT ISSUE: Stellar radiation should push cosmic dust out of the galaxies with continuous acceleration, but the dust content of the galaxy seems to be static. On the other hand, the Poynting-Robertson effect should have swept all cosmic dust into the stars over millions of years, but it is still floating around in our planetary system.

RESPONSE: Stellar explosions seem to be a source of cosmic dust, which then gathers to form more stars or is swept into existing ones. Criticism of these highly speculative evolutionary mechanisms does not constitute proof positive that the cosmos is only six thousand years old.

QUESTION AT ISSUE: Comets also lose material on each

45

pass around the sun. Extrapolation backward would require that a few million years ago their mass was several times that of the sun.

RESPONSE: It is a very tenuous assumption that the same comet visited the sun that often.

QUESTION AT ISSUE: The earth's rotation is slowing down, and again extrapolation backward to billions of years would give the earth such a rapid spin that it would flatten out.

RESPONSE: The motion of the tides transmits a very small part of the earth's angular momentum to the moon, causing a "secular" retardation of the earth's rotation which must be entered into the calculation of eclipses. Various sources give an average figure of .001 second per century, which is 45,000 seconds, or 12.5 hours, in 4.5 billion years. That leaves the early earth with an 11.5-hour day. Jupiter has a 10-hour day, and though it is much larger, its polar diameter is only 7 percent shorter than the equatorial diameter.

The weakness of this extrapolation is that the retardation depends on the distance of the moon, and no one knows where it was at the beginning (cf. Stephen C. Brush, in Godfrey, p. 78). When it was closer, the retardation was greater; so reaching back into time we should find the earth spinning faster than our figures show. But it is hard to see how a more oblate shape of the earth would interfere with its early development.

QUESTION AT ISSUE: Large stars with their rapid nuclear reactions would have disappeared within a few million years.

RESPONSE: According to the astronomers, that is correct — in a few million years.

QUESTION AT ISSUE: These same stellar processes should have used up all the hydrogen in the universe by this time.

46

RESPONSE: Why? Moderate evolution supposes a beginning of the universe, a long time ago.

• Conclusion

What is the verdict? If this had been a live debate, the creationists would not have received my vote. I find their case little better than that of the flat-earthists and geocentrists.

Nevertheless they would have won this debate, as they did most of the others. Why? Because after presenting all the evidence for a young earth, they would have said that the age of the earth is not important anyway, or that it is important for evolution but not for creation. That is the burden of the sixth chapter of *What Is Creation Science?* by Henry Morris, who won all his debates. In the heat of battle a little irrelevant rhetoric scores points: "For evolutionists to concentrate their criticism mostly on this independent issue is merely an admission of the weakness of evolutionism" (p. 219). Of course the date of creation is "an important related issue" (p. 220). But "it will never be possible to *prove* the age of the earth or the universe, of course, since these are matters of history (or 'prehistory') rather than science. . . . We cannot repeat the origin of the earth in the laboratory." So the evolutionist, loser of the debate by popular acclaim, goes home muttering in his beard and may well muse about the following points.

First, if we cannot "prove" anything in history because it cannot be repeated in the laboratory, as the creationists triumphantly insist, then the range of human knowledge is narrow indeed. The laboratory test for hypotheses is a key element in physical science, but it is only a special application, germane to a limited field, of the general source of knowledge, which is observation and evidence. History, prehistory, or for that matter astronomy,

47

are also sciences. Evidence, duly weighed and counter-checked, makes their conclusions as humanly certain as those of physics. We can be as confident that Lincoln was president, or that there were dinosaurs, as that water boils at a constant temperature, even though only the last case can be tested in the laboratory.

Second, a young earth may not be essential to creation — it is not considered so by moderate evolutionists who also insist on creation — but it is essential to creation*ism*. This whole dispute started between Darwinism and six-day literalists. If the young earth is now only "important in its own right" quite independently of the question of creation or evolution, and if we should "consider and teach all the evidence of age, whether old or young, allowing students and others to judge their relative merits for themselves," then the whole game has been changed without warning. But if creationists still insist on their six-day interpretation of Genesis, then they can prove their point scientifically only by proving scientifically that the earth is young. This they have surely failed to do.

At first the scientific world brushed off creation science as a trivial nuisance. Scientists were not expected to waste time refuting flat-earthists, so why should they bother with this? But when they saw that creationists were gaining a hold on the public, there began to appear angry titles like *Abusing Science, the Case Against Creationism*, by P. Kitcher. Even more devastating is *Christianity and the Age of the Earth*, by geologist and Christian apologist David A. Young.

A perceptive and unbiased panel would surely find the scientific arguments for a six-day creation as inept as the effort of Parallax to change the laws of perspective to shore up his "zetetic" theory of a flat earth. It is obvious that this desperate grasping at straws is undertaken, not to learn

48

what happened in history — creationists say we cannot "prove" what happened in the past anyway — but to justify an interpretation of the Bible whose fundamentalist rigidity is, except for a few isolated precedents, a recent phenomenon. We share the concern of Saint Augustine that such a devious use of science only provokes more sneers at our sacred Scriptures. If they are read as the Catholic Church reads them, none of this is necessary, as we shall see further.

Creationists, however, are not only doing battle for their six-day interpretation but are engaged in an all-out war against evolution, so to evolution we now turn.

3

Evolution: Theory and Reality

Evolution means gradual development. The idea of the evolution of the world is at least as old as Confucius, who said that all things "originated from a single simple source through gradual unfolding and branching" (Fothergill, p. 24). In the modern scientific sense it means the gradual, though not necessarily smooth, emergence of the world's features by natural processes working in accordance with natural laws over a long period of time. It includes three major areas: (1) the birth and death of stars in processes that give rise to the chemical elements; (2) the development of the earth's topography; and (3) the development of life.

Subjectively evolution strikes people in different ways. To ardent creationists it is the greatest abomination of the age because they think it excludes creation. They block out any middle ground. Creation and evolution "are antonyms, not synonyms," writes Henry Morris in a moment of semantic confusion (1974, p. 16). *The Truth: God or Evolution* is a title by Marshall and Sandra Hall, and one by Duane Gish is: "It is Either, 'In the Beginning God' . . . or . . . 'Hydrogen.' " On this point they are adamant: evolution cannot be reconciled with creation.

In this fixation they are in complete accord with extreme evolutionists, who would agree with Sir Julian Huxley's statement made in an interview with Irv Kupcinet during the Darwin Centennial celebration in Chicago in 1959: "Darwinism removed the whole idea of God as the creator of organisms from the sphere of rational discussion" (Tax, p. 45). They of course view this divorce not as an abomination but as an emancipation.

It would seem that both sides have removed themselves from the "sphere of rational discussion," and have done so in basically the same way, by insisting that evolution and creation are mutually exclusive. In effect, extreme evolutionists have discovered the evidence for some of the processes and tools by which a house was built and concluded, not very logically, that therefore there was no builder. Creationists show an irrational fear that abandoning the six-day (or "zap") theory of creation in favor of longer natural processes is somehow not only less worthy of the Creator but even eliminates him entirely. Cooler heads of all religious persuasions have long since agreed that evolution and creation are quite compatible. Pun (p. 248) outlines ten compromise steps between the two ex-

51

treme positions, but the most widely accepted Christian position is that evolution is simply the process by which the Creator chose to operate, causing nature to develop according to the laws he created in it.

To steer our way through this topic, we need a few distinctions in the idea of evolution. Many are possible, but the most useful here will be the threefold division into (1) evolution as a natural process, (2) evolution as a theory, and (3) evolution as an ideology. Since the ideology as illustrated by Huxley's statement is parascientific, we leave it to the next chapter. We begin here by viewing evolution "scientifically," looking both at the evidence for the process in nature and at the theory which tries to make sense of the evidence. There are whole shelves of books on evolution, so we touch only a few highlights here.

• The Way of Science

Some say evolution is a "fact," while others, like President Reagan on his first campaign trail, say it is "only a theory." Neither statement should be dismissed, but both should be viewed from a background of what is meant by science and experimental verification. As proposed by Bishop Robert Grosseteste of Lincoln in the thirteenth century and elaborated ever since, the method of science may be divided into four steps: (1) observation; (2) hypothesis, which sees a possible connection between observations and suggests new facts; (3) test of the hypothesis by laboratory experiment or the suggested observation; and (4) acceptance and development of the hypothetical idea as a supported theory or a statement of a law of nature.

We might illustrate this with the example of boiling water, treated partly as history and partly as an idealized thought experiment. People observe that water heated in a vessel comes to a boil. Invention of the thermometer allows the further observation that the boiling temperature is fairly constant. Observation that the boiling temperature is lower at higher elevations leads to the hypothesis that the boiling temperature is constant if the atmospheric pressure is constant. Torricelli's barometer allows a test of this hypothesis and formulation of a partial law: at constant pressure the boiling point of water is constant. This suggests the further hypothesis that all liquids follow this same law, and this also tests out well.

Up to this point there is little "theory" or understanding of why all these "facts" are so, until we hit upon the hypothesis that a liquid boils when its vapor pressure reaches the pressure of the surrounding atmosphere. Direct measurement of vapor pressures confirms this hypothesis, and we now have a small theory, an intellectually satisfying understanding through cause and effect of the constancy of boiling temperatures. The connection between boiling point and pressure is both theory and fact. The theory is the idea in the mind that lends understanding by joining other ideas. Fact is what happens outside the mind, where the connection has been demonstrated. If we now go further and ask why different liquids have diverse boiling points, our hypothesis will lead to the broader theories of atomic structure and bonding and make connections with the laws of thermodynamics.

• Cosmic Evolution

From this easy illustration of the interaction of theory and evidence we may proceed to examine how evolution fits into the scientific scheme, both as an actual process which goes on in nature and as a theory which makes the phenomena intelligible.

If we begin with stellar evolution, we find the factual information in two principal sources, nuclear reactions and astronomical observation. The development of techniques for controlled nuclear reaction in this century has uncovered secrets of matter which seem to lead only to further mysteries in the direction of the very small. But some of the wealth of information can be assembled neatly on a chart of the isotopes of all the elements showing their stability and energy of formation. This is firm evidence, "fact," if you like that term. Like the periodic chart of the elements started by the Russian chemist Mendeleev, it will outlast any adventures in theory.

The second source of evidence is astronomy, and again progress has depended on the development of the telescope and sophisticated techniques and instrumentation. By the method of triangulation for the nearest fixed stars, then through an elaborate study of the spectra of the elements in the stars (the same spectra found in earth laboratories), the stellar distances have been measured, along with stellar size, mass, and surface temperature. This leads to an estimate of the internal conditions of the stars, to their readiness for various nuclear reactions, and to the hypothesis that these reactions take place there. No one will ever visit the inside of a star — at least not using our present technology — to prove that they do, but the most common of these reactions, the conversion of hydrogen to helium, takes place on demand when the H-bomb is primed to several million degrees.

The theory that holds it all together and makes it understandable is an evolutionary one. It is the theory that the stars reached their present state over a period of ten to fifteen billion years by way of the nuclear reactions shown to be plausible by experiments on earth, and that they continue to react and to follow other laws of nature observable on earth. The reality is too far removed in space and time and energy intensity to be directly accessible, but the correspondence with observation gives the theory a high degree of probability.

What is the creationist response? It was all created a few thousand years ago in mid-life, like Adam with his navel, and the indicated development never took place. Einstein may have been wrong about the constancy of the speed of light, so that maybe it takes only about fifteen years for the light from the most distant galaxies to reach us (Morris, 1969, pp. 369-370). Or the red shift may be due, not to the Doppler effect indicating that the stars are receding at greater speed the farther away they are, but just to "tired light" (Sennot, p. 115).

• Evolution of the Earth

Since theory and the discovery of evidence interact in the growth of science, we may reverse ourselves and begin with the theory, namely, that the earth evolved in time to its present state following natural laws and processes still in operation. The story suggested by the theory goes like this:

Some four and a half billion years ago material in flat orbit around the sun was pulled together by gravitation to form the planets, one of which was the earth. The elements combined according to their chemical affinities, the heavy unreacted metals settling to the center and the less dense compounds (especially oxides of silicon, aluminum, calcium, sodium, potassium, iron, and magnesium) remaining near the surface with water. Above them may have been an atmosphere of relatively inert gases: nitrogen, carbon dioxide, and water vapor. Free oxygen was minimal, since it had all combined with the silicon and the metals. Heat was generated by the original compression of the materials, the chemical reactions of the elements, and the radioactivity of the less stable nuclei. The heat was partly trapped beneath the surface, but while radiating gradually into space it also produced internal convection currents, as in hot soup, which over billions of years kept realigning the crust and mantle, allowing for slow crystallization from the melt and isolating pure deposits not only of abundant substances like quartz but also veins of rare elements like gold, concentrating the minerals we now find so useful.

After about two billion years, conditions were right for chemical affinity, essentially no different from that which formed mineral deposits, to carry out the more delicate task of joining carbon, hydrogen, oxygen, nitrogen, phosphorus, and eventually other elements into the metabolizing, self-propagating cell-like aggregates we associate with life. Eventually a photosynthetic form arose which harnessed the energy of the sun to change some of the surface water and most of the carbon dioxide into the oxidizable carbon compounds of plants and free oxygen, a highly reactive element that quickly oxidized all forms of matter, living and nonliving, which could not resist its action.

The continents continued to drift relatively to one another on the convection currents beneath them, pushing up new mountain chains and opening the crust for volcanic action, while the wind and the rain eroded the highlands to peneplains and laid the material on broad plains or in shallow seas.

But in the second half of geological history a new actor had come on the scene. The shallow seas were teeming with living forms, and some of their deposited remains were pushed up by plate collisions to form the highest mountains on earth, like the Himalayas. Other forms of sea life by some as yet obscure mechanism probably produced the petroleum deposits. Swamp plants which were partly protected from oxidation when they fell in shallow water, piled up and were compressed to form coal seams. Changes of climate led to ice ages, and continental ice sheets in more recent epochs have receded to leave such familiar modern features as the Great Lakes, scoured bedrock, moraines, erratics, and eskers. The tale can be expanded into volumes (cf. Ehrensvärd).

If it all sounds like a "fairy tale for grownups," as evolution has been called (Lammerts, 1970, p. 328), it is because evolution fills the gaps between the supports of solid fact with bridges of speculation that the facts suggest. The story keeps changing. The obviously crucial factor of continental drift or plate tectonics has been included by only the latest generation of geologists, and we may be sure there is more to come.

The first factual evidence which stirred the curiosity of the ancients as well as such scholars as Albert the Great and Leonardo da Vinci was the unmistakable trace of sea life far from the sea and high above sea level. The first reaction to such a discovery, beyond a shrug, might be to call it a mystery; but it is hardly a supernatural mystery, and reason doggedly pursues an explanation. A recurrent temptation is to follow Gosse in his *Omphalos* and say that God created Adam with a navel even though he had no mother, the earth to look old when it was not, and the rocks to look like sea deposits when they are not. This is the position to which creationists are driven, and Dobzhansky says (p. 6), "Those who choose to believe that God created every biological species separately in the state we observe them but made them in a way calculated to lead us to the conclusion that they are the products of an evolutionary development are obviously not open to argument. All that can be said is that their belief is an implicit blasphemy, for it imputes to God an appalling deviousness." The verdict seems just, even if the sentence is extreme. Creationists respond by

57

saying that God is like an artist who creates a fully developed world, but the reply is not apropos. God did not create a still-life canvas but a world in process, and the processes point back to an evolutionary history.

As mentioned in the first chapter, the earliest concerted effort to explain seashells in mountain formations was seventeenth-century catastrophism. It has been brought up to date by creationist efforts like *The Genesis Flood* of Morris and Whitcomb. Morris earned his doctorate at the University of Minnesota, majoring in hydraulics in order to be able to show scientifically what he was already convinced of by his interpretation of the Bible, namely that the Deluge could account for the earth's geological features. Of course the Flood did not simply deposit sea-bottom materials on the tops of existing mountains; rather, the mountains are made of them. So the catastrophists have to suppose that the mountains rose quickly from sea bottoms in an orogeny that geologists measure in millions of years. It all happened in the year of the Deluge, on a scale that surely never entered the mind of the human writer of Genesis.

Their strenuous efforts bring out some interesting elements of science fiction but hardly make their thesis believable. Such large-scale catastrophism also conflicts with the second area of evidence for slow evolution, the stratification of sedimentary rocks. When William Smith worked out the relative ages of the English formations in the early part of the nineteenth century, he did not advocate evolution. He first assumed what is called the "law of superposition," namely, the younger sea deposits are normally on top of older ones. Then since complete strata could not be uncovered, he connected them by the "index fossils" of sea life found in them.

Creationists see circular reasoning in this, but there is none. They say the age of rocks is used as a proof of evolu-

58

tion — which is true; and then evolution is used to prove the age of the rocks — which is not true, even though evolutionist writers sometimes carelessly assume that it is (cf. Morris, 1963, p. 51). Whether the "index fossils" are simpler or more advanced, more "evolved," than those in other strata makes no difference. They are simply a "funny mark" (Raup, in Godfrey, p. 154) characteristic of one era and lacking in another. Relative age estimates were based on superposition. There was no scale for determining absolute time accurately, but it surely exceeded the six thousand years of the biblical literalists. The Mississippian limestone deposits reach two thousand feet in thickness and the sea animals they represent could hardly all have been living in the year of the Flood.

The third kind of evidence for the evolutionary story of the earth is the "absolute" though often not very precise time scale provided by radioactivity. The oldest of these methods, based on the Rutherford-Fajans-Soddy series of reactions reducing uranium or thorium to stable isotopes of lead, is quite straightforward in the idealized world of pure substances on which chemical science depends. Minerals tend to form crystals of one kind of molecule, though they may be quite complex. In the long Precambrian cooling-off period, when rocks were reburied, twisted, and metamorphosed, even rare elements (which include most of the ninety-two) managed to collect in high enough concentrations to be usable ores in human times.

Uranium crystallized in a number of forms, of which pitchblende, U_3O_8, is the richest in uranium. U-238, which is the principal isotope, disintegrates spontaneously by loss of an alpha particle, and has a half-life of four and a half billion years, determined in effect by counting the rate of alpha emission of a pure sample. The daughter products, the nine elements between uranium and lead, are all radioactive, and they collect in the mineral at an equilibrium concentration which is proportional to their stability. It was from a large quantity of pitchblende that the Curies first isolated a small sample of polonium and another of radium. The final product of this series of reactions is lead-206. Ideally no lead should have crystallized with the pitchblende, so the time elapsed since the crystallization of the mineral is calculated directly from the ratio of lead to uranium in the sample.

But nature rarely serves up pure chemical substances. Water is the only one we encounter daily that is naturally pure enough to display the constant properties of a chemical substance, such as melting point, density, and the like. If we know where to look, we can find various pure salts, sugar, carbon as charcoal and diamond, and the vast array of minerals which crystallized out of the melt. If anyone is prepared to account for impure substances as departures from the ideal, it is the chemist, including the nuclear chemist. Most of the efforts of the creationists to discredit calculations of the great age of the earth consist in pointing to the efforts of scientists to account for discrepancies, for non-ideality. A check of the literature cited by the creationists will invariably show that the scientists were quite aware of the problems and knew where they were going (cf. Godfrey).

Many factors could alter the results of uranium-lead dating. U-235, besides fissioning under bombardment by neutrons in atomic power production and bombs, also emits alpha particles and starts its own series leading to lead-207. But U-235 is less than one percent of natural uranium, so the error would be small even if neglected. Then the separation in the early crystallization was seldom ideal. Uranium minerals may contain lead, so it is necessary first to determine the ratio of nonradiogenic isotope

60

lead-204 to lead-206, 207, and 208, which may be the products of radioactivity, and compare them with ratios in lead deposits far removed from uranium. These things are done without prompting from creationists, and when all is said, the age of the oldest mineral thus far discovered is about 3.8 billion years.

There are a half dozen more methods, each with its own problems and its own niche. The potassium-argon method has the advantage that potassium is abundant and ubiquitous and has one rather rare radioactive isotope. Argon, the product, is a gas, so care is needed to see that none has escaped or been added from another source.

Creationists contend that decay rates are not constant, but no fluctuation has been found in laboratory experience. One of the earliest observations about radioactive decay was that it was not affected in any way by physical changes or chemical processes. Creationists suggest that cosmic rays or neutrinos may speed up the rate. But in physics everything has its price. If nuclear bombardment produces an effect, as when cosmic rays strike the upper atmosphere, the energy is used up before it reaches the mineral deposits of the earth. If neutrinos penetrate deep it is because their reactions are very improbable. Experience with radioactive dating is sufficiently advanced so that the age of the earth stands at a minimum of four and a half billion years and anthropological-archaeological finds can be dated within an acceptable margin of error.

• Biological Evolution

To justify the adage that there is nothing new under the sun, we begin our treatment of the evolution of living things with A.C. Crombie's summary of what the ancients thought on the subject (pp. 118-119):

Anaximander held that all life had originated by

spontaneous generation from water and that man had developed from fish. Xenophanes quoted fossil fish and seaweed as evidence that life arose from mud. Empedocles believed that life arose by spontaneous generation from earth; first plants appeared and then parts of animals (including man), heads, arms, eyes, etc., which united by chance and produced forms of all sorts, monstrous or proper. The proper forms extinguished the monstrous and, when the sexes had become differentiated, reproduced themselves, and the earth then ceased its generation. . . .

Apart from Anaximander's all these theories accounted for the succession of new species, not by modification from living ancestors, but by generation from a common source such as the earth. But some ancient writers, such as Theophrastus, had believed that existing types were sometimes mutable. Albertus accepted this belief and illustrated it by the domestication of wild plants and the running wild of domesticated plants. . . .

Speculations about the origin of new species and mutation of those now existing continued . . . with Henry of Hesse (1325-97), who referred to the appearance of new diseases and new herbs which would be needed to cure them. Later they entered the natural philosophies of Bruno, who was indebted also to the Stoics, and of Francis Bacon, Leibniz, and the evolutionists of the 18th century. The reflections of Albertus Magnus and of Henry of Hesse on the mutation of species were not related to any concept of an evolving, developing and progressing universe, animal kingdom, or human race, an idea which is characteristically modern and had no place in medieval thought.

62

The evidence for biological evolution falls into three categories. The first is the morphology (that is, the anatomy or the makeup) of things living now, on which Darwin's argument in the *Origin of Species* is chiefly grounded. He lays out in endless detail the evidence that plants and animals nearly alike vary more or less according to the locale, and that the variations are inherited. The varieties of pigeons provide him a favorite example. The longer the environment has been isolated, the more the flora and fauna differ. Australia is a good example here. There is direct evidence for slight changes in organisms — microevolution this is called — from garden plants to wild birds like the finches Darwin studied on the Galapagos Islands. We note that modern evolution is partly a product of the world explorations by Europeans after the fifteenth century.

A second line of evidence is found in common anatomical features. Animals inherit four limbs with five digits each. Monkeys use all twenty digits to advantage. We use our toes very little as digits. Horses use four digits, the rest being vestigial. Common ancestry is an answer to the question "Why?" A horse with sixteen unused digits is an embarrassment to the theory that each species was created separately.

Other common functional parts reach into more distinct classes and phyla; for example, the skeleton of vertebrates and chlorophyll in plants. Most striking is the fact that the whole biosphere — plant and animal — shares the same basic DNA molecule as a template for reproduction of cells. (DNA, as you may recall, is the acronym for deoxyribonucleic acid, the chief genetic material that determines what characteristics a living organism will inherit.)

The third line of evidence is found in the fossil record. The hard fact is that rocks dated as Precambrian show little sign of life, Cambrian and Ordovician rocks contain simple life-forms, and the more elaborate "higher" forms come later. While no entire phylum has disappeared, some forms have. Trilobites vanished three hundred million years ago and dinosaurs fifty million years ago.

• Evolutionary Theory

This overall factual information fits neatly into the general theory that all life evolved by direct reproductive descent from one kind. The only alternative theory proposed so far is separate creation. This means that the different forms are not genetically related, that the new varieties we see emerging never reach the level of separate biological species, that the species were created separately for each environment, and that the species which existed in the past reproduced without change and then suddenly died out. This theory can force some of the facts to fit, but it is untidy, ignoring secondary causes and natural processes, unworthy of the unity and order found in nature. To defend their theory, creationists are driven to deny what we have called the "facts," especially the evidence that the earth is very old and that species lived at different times. When we compare it with evolutionary theory, we can only conclude that separate creation theory would have no standing whatsoever except for the erroneous opinion that it was revealed by the Creator.

But evolutionary theory must move on from generality to particulars. It must try to explain what makes the process go, and this is where difficulties arise. In Neo-Darwinian theory the mechanism usually includes three parts.

The first is natural selection, emphasized by Darwin after he took his cue from the thesis of Malthus that living populations tend to increase exponentially until checked by natural restraints such as lack of food, the presence of predators, and unfavorable climate. Which living things survive the natural restraints and keep their species going? The fittest, answers Darwin, borrowing the expression, "survival of the fittest" from the evolutionist-philosopher Herbert Spencer. "Struggle for existence" is found in the subtitle of Darwin's *Origin of Species*, and is the third of the somewhat controversial expressions connected with Darwinism. Extreme evolutionists should be uncomfortable with the fact that selection implies choice in a process they consider purely mechanical. "Survival of the fittest," after serving as a slogan for Hitlerism and the robber barons of industry, has been muted to "survival of the fit to survive," or something equally inane. Nature does not always select the best specimens to survive. When a bird's nest is robbed, the best eggs have the same chance of being eaten as the worst. Life is not always a struggle for existence; and, in times of stress, fitness to survive hunger and hardship may not exist in the same individual as fitness to evade predators or find food. Survival of the species hinges on mating prowess, helped by big antlers or bright colors, which may be a handicap to individual survival.

Yet no matter what we call it, we see something like natural selection in operation, especially when we have to look for a new insecticide because one strain of bug was resistant to the old and multiplied quickly to take over the field. Natural selection is a "fact" and a law of nature as inexorable as gravity. How well it can explain evolution is another matter.

The second causal factor is variation. It is really first in the order of things, but Darwin was unable to deal with it, writing, as he did, before Mendel's laws of heredity had been rediscovered and accepted at the turn of the century. To the negative factor, elimination by natural selection,

65

modern evolutionary theory adds a positive source of variation in offspring through the operation of the laws of genetics and through accidental mutation, by either chemical or nuclear interaction, of the genes situated in the nucleic acids of the gametes, or reproductive cells.

A third causal factor is reproductive isolation, in which new varieties evolving must be prevented from interbreeding with the old. Then the altered gene can be passed on to the offspring through the highly accurate process of cell regeneration.

• Survival of the Theory

Is evolution becoming extinct, as creationists claim wishfully? To estimate its survival prospect we may take another lesson from history.

The geocentric Ptolemaic theory of the motion of heavenly bodies was based on the older Greek idea that these heavenly bodies were of different substance than earth so they would not fall, and that they moved only in perfect circular paths. Astronomy was an important science in antiquity, and the theory did what a scientific theory is supposed to do: it provided a model and system of ideas that made the observed changes in the sky understandable, and it served a useful purpose in the regulation of the calendar and the prediction of eclipses. For over a thousand years this system of epicycles was elaborated by learned men to account for more and more detail until finally Copernicus revived the heliocentric idea and Galileo trained his new telescope on the earthly mountains of the moon, showing that the old theory, for all its elegance and usefulness, turned reality inside out. But the observations of the position and movements of the heavenly bodies remained valid and had to be accounted for by the new theory.

The phlogiston theory of combustion of the eighteenth

century is a similar case. It did not survive as long as the geocentric theory, but was accepted by scientists at least half as long as modern evolution. It accounted for appearances. Combustible materials were supposed to be made up of phlogiston and ash. When they burned, the phlogiston departed in the flame, leaving the ash. Lavoisier eventually showed that it was a completely backward model of nature by demonstrating that combustion involved not a loss of substance but a gain, through combination of the combustible material with the oxygen of the air. Great experimenters like Black, Priestley, and Scheele were phlogistonists who made giant strides in isolating pure chemical substances. Again their factual contribution stands. The caloric theory of heat suffered a similar inversion.

Other theories have changed less dramatically. The ancient atomic theory that matter was made up of discrete particles was demonstrated conclusively only in the twentieth century, but the part about the *atomos*, the impenetrable, indivisible particle, proved to be an illusion. The atomic theory remains central, however, as does Newton's theory of gravitation, even though the latter has been absorbed in the more comprehensive theory of relativity.

Will the theory of evolution also prove to be a reversed picture of nature? Not likely. The overall developmental pattern in nature is as well established as anything else in history. But as time goes on, the incompleteness of the theory becomes more evident, as it does with all scientific theories that are still extant. Some of these shortcomings will be considered later. For now we shall look at two specific objections.

• The Missing Link
The hoariest of these is the missing link. Darwin constructed his theory with little reliance on the scant fossil

evidence available to him. But if evolution actually took place, if it is a historical fact, then a record of the past should be an important support when added to the evidence of the relatedness of present forms of life.

Creationist-debater Duane Gish wrote a book called *Evolution? The Fossils Say No!* In fact the fossils say nothing of the kind. The abundance of fossil evidence obtained over the past century demonstrates beyond the shadow of reasonable doubt that forms of life existed in the past which are now extinct and that new species now thrive which did not exist in earlier geological periods. Equally clear is the overall trend toward "higher," more complex life-forms in the passage of time, especially the trend toward more sophisticated brains. The pattern exposed by the fossil evidence is therefore one of evolution in the broad sense. Fossils allow us to speak of the evolution of life with as much conviction as we speak, say, of the development of civilization.

What is lacking is direct evidence that the higher forms are the offspring of the lower, which is evolution in a more specific sense. There is of course no direct evidence that life proceeded in any other way. The lack of direct evidence is supplied by the theory, from an understanding of how life processes work, and faulty interpretation is always possible.

Any other historical study is subject to the same limitations. The record supplies a few highlights. What people are doing most of the time we can surmise in a general way from our knowledge of human life, but this is not recorded and most particulars are lost forever. They are missing links. Still we can achieve human certainty about the major events of history. It is unlikely that a maverick historian would be able to convince us that President Woodrow Wilson and King George III were contemporaries. It is equally unlikely that creationists will be able to convince us that dinosaurs and Adam were contemporaries.

The missing-link objection begins to look weak when we consider that nearly all the links in the fossil record of the history of life are necessarily missing. If everything that lived in the past five hundred million years had been preserved in fossil forms, the mass of fossil rock would far outweigh the earth. In that hypothetical case no links would be missing, but there would still be no direct evidence that one denizen was the ancestor of another. Prize animals and humans have pedigrees and records of parentage, but not wildlife.

Furthermore, fossilization is a very specialized and rare process. To be preserved for an appreciable geological period, an animal or plant must fall where it will be covered and where water can seep through at the proper rate to leach out corruptible material and replace it with siliceous or calcareous material, changing it to stone. Petrified wood is familiar to us, and its rarity is typical of fossils formed away from the sea. Over two hundred thousand fossil species have been classified, but since there are about two million species living now and the average survival time of a species is only a fraction of the two billion years of life on earth, it is easy to see that most species are missing from the fossil record. Among those on the record many are recognizable as intermediate forms, but the evolutionist would appreciate more of the critical ones, like fossil evidence for the division of life into the plant and animal kingdoms.

Fossil evidence can yield only a varying degree of probability that one particular species descended from another, the horse from the eohippus, for example. Wolfgang Smith (p. 67) and others of the same mind are therefore correct in saying that evolution is not directly verifiable by paleontology, since the fossils show sequence but not filiation, or descent from a particular ancestry. But the implication that therefore filiation did not take place is not justified. The fossil evidence fits the theory of evolution by filiation well, and is unintelligible without it. Creationists say their model predicts the gaps in the fossil record. Their problem is that it predicts only the gaps, not the fossils.

• Evolution and Thermodynamics

We should not close this treatment of evolution and its discontents without referring to a major creationist claim: evolution is impossible because it violates the inexorable laws of thermodynamics. The first law of thermodynamics is that the total energy, including that from the transformation of mass into energy, in any closed system is constant. The second law is that the availability of energy to do work always decreases in any irreversible process in a closed system; that is, entropy or unavailability or randomness always increases and never decreases in a closed system.

Henry Morris claims that evolutionists do not understand the second law, or entropy (1963, p. 33), which is the result of the curse of Eden (p. 37). He devotes thirty-six pages (153-188) of his 1982 book *What Is Creation Science?* to setting their minds straight. A reader with some acquaintance with thermodynamics will find the argument less beguiling than the average reader, but anyone should be able to mark the following points:

1. Morris reiterates the creationist theme that "the Second Law of thermodynamics is especially significant in its support of the creation model, and correspondingly, its contradiction of the evolution model" (p. 164). Everything goes downhill and wears out. "This experience of deterioration is so universal and so common that it is surprising that anyone could ever believe in evolution" (p. 165).

70

2. Again and again scientists have remonstrated with the creationists: It is not all downhill! Entropy can decrease in a system like the earth which is open to outside energy from the sun. So on page 172, apparently unaware that he is reneging on the sweeping statement of page 165, Morris answers that "no knowledgeable creationist ever says that all systems go downhill. One can even make water flow uphill — by putting a pump in the line. . . . Living systems . . . do indeed manifest, for a time, an increasing degree of complexity . . . without in any way breaking the Second Law . . . at the expense of the overall increase in entropy in a larger system outside. . . . But these cases are exceptions . . . and thus require particular explanations."

One would hardly call plant and animal life exceptions. They belong to the regular order of nature and they increase the amount of available energy in one part of nature at the expense of an increased entropy in the closed solar system. The sun is of course running down and in a few billion years more could be useless to us. A non-biological example of decreasing entropy is the evaporation of water into the atmosphere where it is available to fall as rain, and, with further machinery, to do useful work. In principle, then, creationists and evolutionists are again of one mind: entropy can be reversed.

3. Morris lists four conditions for increasing complexity and decreasing entropy: (a) a system open to outside energy; (b) a source of that energy; (c) a program to direct the growth, like DNA and chlorophyll in living systems; and (d) a mechanism like photosynthesis or metabolism or man-made machinery. He claims that the directing program and conversion mechanism "are available in such cases as the growth of plants or the erection of a building, but not in the supposed billion-year evolution of the biosphere" (p. 187).

This is a gratuitous distinction. Biologists cite photosynthesis as the mechanism in plant growth, and variation and natural selection for evolution. To say that there is a mechanism in one case but not the other is unwarranted. But under the mistaken impression that he is still talking thermodynamics and arguing from rigorous physical laws, Morris has brought the question around to where it should be and where most evolutionists would put it: Is the Neo-Darwinian mechanism of mutation, selection, and isolation an adequate one?

Criticism of the theory within the ranks has centered recently not on the inadequacy of natural selection but on the assumption that evolution is entirely gradual. The battle of the gaps has led to an updated version of the saltation theory. That of Eldredge and Gould is called punctuated equilibrium. It postulates long periods of stasis within species, punctuated by occasional periods of more rapid but still evolutionary growth. It is of course an adjustment within the theory, not an abandonment of the idea of evolution.

The overall pattern of evolution will not go away. But the creationist attack — as well as misgivings within the ranks — calls our attention to shortcomings of Neo-Darwinian theory and to the abuses that have entered into the study of evolution.

4

The Theory Abused — Ideology

The theory of evolution viewed straight on is a way of understanding how the physical and biological world passed from young to old, a scientific study of development. But in real life, scientific theories often fail to keep their place. They become swollen into what for lack of a better term we may call an ideology, a whole way of life riding on one idea. A modest and serviceable idea grows too big for its backyard and extends its tentacles to all of reality, reducing everything to its terms. Julian Huxley again puts it with naïve candor: "all reality is a single process of evolution" (Tax, p. 294). Evolution is not the first scientific theory to lose its innocence in this fashion. To observe the trend we must look back into history once more.

The atomic theory, which is also an evolutionary one, arose in the late fifth century B.C., shortly after the great watershed in human thought that saw the rise of Confucianism and Taoism in China, Buddhism in India, Zoroastrianism in Persia (modern-day Iran), and the beginnings of Greek philosophy out of the realization that the world could be understood in terms of reasoned laws without recourse to the mysterious spirits of animism. Atomism is found in India, but it influenced the West in the version of Leucippus and his better-known follower Democritus.

Departing from the view of Parmenides that all reality is permanent and change an illusion, Democritus saw the one permanent reality as divided into tiny atoms of different shapes moving through the void. Even though direct experimental verification would have to wait another twenty-four centuries, it was a proper scientific theory, a way of understanding the observed physical states of matter and physical and chemical change in terms of the common behavior of matter. It was artfully used in this way by Democritus and later by the Roman poet Lucretius.

But starting as it did from a universal metaphysics, it quickly outran its leash and took in all of reality. It was reductionist, reducing all to atoms. This quotation comes down to us from Democritus: "According to convention there is a sweet and a bitter, a hot and a cold, and according to convention there is color. In truth there are [only] atoms and a void" (Dampier, p. 23).

There is an age-old dispute about whether secondary qualities like sweetness and color are real in the object, as in an apple in a dark room with nobody to eat it, or only in the subject who sees and tastes it. The sensible solution

74

would seem to be to give each its due, but Democritus said that only atoms and the space they move in are real, just as modern reductionists say that only electromagnetic waves are real and color exists only in the mind (Ditfurth, p. 138). Atomism gives everything else the same treatment. If there is a soul, it must be made of very "subtle" atoms, material ones to be able to influence a material body.

Plato and Aristotle had little use for all this, even though they both speculated on the "smallest" parts. Modern writers generally chide them for retarding the progress of natural science by rejecting the atomic theory, but they should first blame those who warped the theory with their materialistic bias.

For over two thousand years atomic theory has been obliged to carry a threefold ideological burden: materialism, atheism, and determinism. Nothing is supposed to exist except the material atoms, which in antiquity were arbitrarily assigned the properties of eternity and "infinity" so that the Creator was dispensed with. The Epicureans embraced this cosmology. Later some Islamic philosophers accepted atomism, and while they thought of atoms as created, they accepted the determinism. If man is made up of atoms, little automatons moved by rigid physical laws, he cannot be blamed for his behavior.

Galileo, Boyle, and Newton, among many others, speculated on atoms and tried to keep the theory trimmed down to size. Sir Isaac Newton, who expended about as much effort in his lifetime on theology as on physics, was especially circumspect: "It seems probable to me, that God in the beginning, form'd Matter in solid, massy, hard, impenetrable, moveable Particles, of such Sizes and Figures, and with such other Properties, and in such Proportion to Space, as most conduced to the End for which he form'd them" (*Optiks*, in Taylor, p. 142).

In 1737 Daniel Bernoulli made a brilliant yet quite sober derivation of Boyle's law of the inverse proportionality of pressure and volume in gases from the new laws of mechanics operating on "corpuscles" of atomic dimensions.

Elsewhere enthusiasm swept modesty aside, as in the famous remark of Laplace that "a superhuman intelligence acquainted with the position and motion of the atoms at any moment could predict the whole course of future events" (Burtt, p. 96). This was before the discovery of subatomic particles and electromagnetism, and before twentieth-century relativity led to the equally exaggerated view that everything is relative, and quantum theory suggested that position and motion viewed simultaneously are indeterminate and intrinsically unknowable.

But throughout the nineteenth century there was no foreboding of such chilling events, and materialism and determinism held the field. The deistic idea was that the Creator had originally launched the machinery of the world, but soon the Creator was also abandoned by the wayside. Another story about Laplace is as famous as the one given above. When he presented his book on celestial mechanics to Napoleon, someone told the emperor that God was not mentioned in it. When Napoleon twitted Laplace about this, the answer was, "I have no need of that hypothesis" (Dampier, p. 181).

From its Greek beginnings atomism included evolution. Following the cyclic model of many ancient pagan cosmogonies, the eternal atoms were supposed to have evolved into endless worlds, with more to come. It was only to be expected that from the middle of the nineteenth century evolution and Darwin's work should be enlisted to support atheistic ideologies, including Marxism.

Darwin himself in his *Origin of Species* occasionally

refers to the "works of God" and the "works of the Creator," and his intention was not to exclude him but to discredit "separate and innumerable acts of creation." Later in life he descended to the agnostic stage if not beyond, not because he thought evolution made the world self-sufficient but because it confronted him with endless ages of animal suffering which he found incompatible with a sensitive Creator. Darwin tells us: "A being so powerful and full of knowledge as a God who could create the universe, is to our finite minds omnipotent and omniscient, and it revolts our understanding to suppose that his benevolence is not unbounded, for what advantage can there be in the sufferings of millions of the lower animals throughout almost endless time?" (*Autobiography*, p. 90).

It is an ancient chestnut. Two thousand years ago Lucretius wrote in *De Rerum Natura*: "Suppose I were ignorant and did not know what atoms are. I would still make bold to claim from my observation of the ways of heaven and from many other things that this world of ours was not prepared for us by any god. Too much is wrong with it. . . ."

One response is the philosophical consideration that a created world cannot be perfect. To be perfect it would need the inherent perfection of self-existence and so would not need to be created. So a created world is necessarily imperfect. But such a cold theory does not soothe the feelings.

On the list of those who used evolution in their war against religion is Thomas Huxley, the biologist-debater who cut down the Anglican Bishop Wilberforce in the most famous of all debates on evolution. For Huxley evolution has as ". . . one of its greatest merits . . . the fact that it occupies a position of complete and irreconcilable antagonism to that vigorous and consistent enemy of mankind, the Catholic Church" (Fothergill, p. 13).

Karl Marx was so favorably impressed with Darwin's work that he offered to dedicate *Das Kapital* to him, but Darwin demurred. Apparently Stalin was still in ecclesiastical school when he read Darwin and became an atheist (Lammerts, 1971, p. 341). Countless others, like Andrew Carnegie (Boller, p. 54), followed Darwin into agnosticism.

It is not hard to understand the pull on adolescent minds of simple theories like evolution and Tinker-toy atomism. In an instant of easy enlightenment everything in the universe is understood, and with the divine Judge swept out of the picture, the moral difficulties associated with growing up can be faced with a profound sense of relief.

Perhaps it is to such immature escapism along with an adolescent inability to see the limits of an idea that we should ascribe some of the astonishing statements that reach us from evolutionary ideology. In addition to Julian Huxley's classic about evolution excluding the Creator from rational discussion, here are a few gems from famous authors who shall be left nameless out of respect for the living:

✓ In the beginning . . . life assembled itself.

✓ If the mind has no real existence beyond the brain, can God be anything more than an illusion invented by an illusion?

✓ Man knows at last that he is alone in the universe's unfeeling immensity, out of which he emerged only by chance.

✓ Man's evolutionary journey has prepared him to face life and the universe with acceptance in the face of meaninglessness and hope in the face of ignorance.

Evolutionary ideology is not confined to atheists. Father Pierre Teilhard de Chardin's sweeping view of everything on the way to the Omega Point is surely an ideology in the meaning we have been following.

On the other hand, if an author begins with a more universal principle or idea instead of a scientific theory, we call his work a philosophy. Hegel's was an evolutionary philosophy according to which the Absolute is in infinite process, becoming successively nature and spirit. In England in 1857, two years before Darwin's *Origin of Species* came out, Herbert Spencer published *Progress, Its Law and Cause,* in which the principle of evolution was enunciated as a universal law which is followed by nature, the mind, and society. He helped to popularize Darwinism, especially in America, and a sequel to his thought is the idea of social Darwinism and the survival of the master races and of the economically fit against the poor and the weak. In Germany Haeckel promoted a materialistic, evolutionary monism (that is, that the only reality is matter in evolution), and in France Henri Bergson revived the claim of Heraclitus that only change is real. He departs from mechanistic evolution by supposing an "élan vital," a live urge in the world which keeps evolution from grinding to a halt and drives it onward and upward to the level of consciousness. Process philosophies and existentialism follow somewhat parallel paths, and the strained dictum that "man is evolution become conscious of itself" is reminiscent of the existentialist identification of man with his own freedom.

Creationists charge that evolution is a religion, and inasmuch as evolution is the cosmology of secular humanism, which is defined as a religion in its manifestos of 1933 and 1973, signed by a number of professors of religion and ministers, it is a part of the religion of some. But if we define religion as the relation of man to God, then any religion without God is only a hollow psychological, ethical, and ritual shell that remains after the heart is cut out, a mere travesty of the name of religion.

But in this truncated sense secular humanism has it

all: for the Creator, Evolution; for Heaven, Posterity and Human Progress; for Faith, "a positive declaration in times of uncertainty." In ethics it declares for the rights of all peoples in a world community, while advocating tolerance of diversity in "life-styles" and expressions of "sexual proclivities," no matter how inhuman. It professes concern for the disadvantaged while advocating anti-life policies — abortion, euthanasia, the right to suicide — which would disencumber the world of their presence.

Its ritual is a tedious sermon, a prophetic admonition to conserve nature and stop pollution, with apocalyptic warnings about the population bomb and the nuclear holocaust. Christians accept the divine commission given through Adam to be stewards of creation. They may have failed that moral obligation as they do others, but preachers who reject the divine foundation are blowing into the wind.

Modern evolution, modern psychology, and sociology were born with a deadly canker inherited from their founders who for all their original contributions to particular fields of knowledge furthered the headlong decline of human and spiritual values in the nineteenth century. It is still not easy to sort out the positive contribution from the dry rot in which it grew up. Atomic theory took an even longer time to emerge pure from its noxious cloud.

• Limitations of the Theory

Even without the ideological barnacles, the theory of evolution is still beset with what we may call, in Cardinal Newman's memorable phrase, "the logical insufficiency of Mr. Darwin's theory" (Vol. 25, p. 446), and Neo-Darwinism has not entirely filled the gap. Darwin's idea was essentially that life evolved because less favorable variants were filtered out by natural selection. Neo-Darwinism clarified the source of variations: breeding according to Mendel's laws, accidental mutation, with reproductive isolation to keep things going in the same direction. All except creationists agree that four billion years ago there was an earth without life, that now we have all kinds of plants and animals and people communicating sophisticated ideas throughout the world and beyond, and that the passage from the first state to the second was slow and fairly gradual. Mechanistic evolutionists may avoid speaking of "higher" forms of life, but it is pretty obvious that human beings have something positive that vegetables do not have.

The question remains: How do these three factors produce an upward movement leading to higher forms of life? Natural selection is essentially negative. The weaker forms succumb under conditions of stress while the more fit survive and propagate. The causes of selection, such as scarcity and competition, are destructive and add nothing to what the specimens already have. Dobzhansky (pp. 154-155) distinguishes normalizing selection, which has the negative role of eliminating detrimental mutants, from directional or dynamic selection, "which alters the genetic composition of a population in response to a changing or changed environment." But it would seem that if dynamic selection alters the genetic composition of a population merely by eliminating nonadaptive forms, it is still negative; it does not supply the adaptive forms. If selection in this passive sense is creative, as evolutionists say, it is so only indirectly. We are still looking for a sufficient reason for the upward movement to more complex and self-contained life, toward greater intelligence, and toward such things as beauty in butterfly wings. Passive selection alone is surely not it, even though it is unassailable as a natural law controlling populations and evolution.

To selection Neo-Darwinism adds the laws of genetics based on the DNA pattern. In bisexual generation the two

81

genotypes are crossed and the genes passed on to the progeny. The genetic mechanism allows recognizable traits to be inherited. It is not as though blue paint were mixed with yellow and the individual colors lost forever. The offspring of a blonde and a brunette can be blonde. But the old genes are only mixed. No new ones are supplied.

Where do the favorable variations come from? Neo-Darwinists invoke random mutation of the DNA of sperm or ovum, in a process that is about as constructive as a shotgun blast. Some rare mutations may be favorable, and defenders of this aspect of the theory say that natural selection eliminates the defective offspring and allows the rare improvement to be inherited. But a nagging doubt remains. In a single generation in a limited population, chances are that all mutations will be unfavorable, leaving offspring worse or at least not better off than the parents. Under conditions of stress the weaklings will be eliminated, but the survivors will still be at an inferior average level, and any favorable mutation in the future will have to build on that inferior base. Evolution which relies solely on passive natural selection looks like steady deterioration.

Would some kind of active selection save the day? Darwin invoked it heavily when he argued for natural evolution by pointing to the improvements brought about by the domestic breeding of plants and animals, an old and successful human enterprise carried out by intelligent planners to enhance desirable characteristics. But this brings in an active agent outside the plant or animal subject, and so it is artificial rather than natural selection.

Orthodox Neo-Darwinists are rather reticent about active natural selection, selection by the subject to be improved rather than by environmental forces; but occasionally their language points in that direction, as when Dobzhansky speaks of dynamic selection in "response" to an environmental change. Monod says that an organism "snaps up" the rare favorable mutations (p. 123), and Eldredge says "the species tracks the change" and the "environment provides the opportunity for a species to invent the truly new" (p. 133). Ernst Mayr writes: "As soon as selection is defined as differential reproduction, its creative aspects become evident" (p. 202). He then illustrates this by comparing it to pulling C.A.T. out of a bag of letters by random drawing, discarding all other letters until those three are obtained. He is obviously implying that something besides the bag of letters is doing the selecting, and by analogy, some active selective principle is involved in differential reproduction.

In fact we observe this active selection at every level. Two molecules of water select each other to begin an ice crystal. The ice crystal selects water molecules and rejects all other kinds, and water molecules have an affinity for an already formed ice crystal. Active selection is even more apparent in living things. Organisms select nourishment and reject what is useless. The active response of an organism to the environment seems as important to evolution as the action of the environment on the organism.

If the organism snaps up the favorable mutation, much as it selects food and rejects harmful bacteria or cancerous cells, then the quicksand aspect of merely passive selection is circumvented and we can see how evolution can move forward. But this view requires that we look first at the organism as a whole, that we see the entire unit as more fundamental than the assemblage of parts, as we think of a house first as a dwelling place, as a whole which determines the arrangement of lumber. This is a point of view favored by biologists like Adolf Portman of Basel and others cited by Mynarek, as well as philosophers and theologians like Herman Schell. But its contribution to the scientific theory of evolution remains problematic. As we shall see in the chapter on creation, it points directly to design and purpose in nature, and to that extent is anathema to the reductionist temper of extreme evolutionism.

Nevertheless passive selection seems to have been the stumbling block to acceptance of evolution from the beginning, so that the theory is continually being reinforced by what Monod (Ch. 2) complains of as a plague of "vitalistic" and "animistic" supplements. Henri Bergson introduced the "élan vital," and Teilhard de Chardin a "radial" or ascending energy. "To this day, French biologists prefer some sort of directed evolution" (Hull, p. 153). Ninety-five percent of them reject Darwinism (Mayr, p. 309; Litynski). You may say that they are being chauvinistic, or you may say that Darwinism offends the logical French mind. These are Lamarck's countrymen, as well as Monod's. But in England also, Spencer wrote of an unknowable force, and in Germany Driesch proposed vitalism, a force beyond matter. Marx borrowed Hegel's world mind, and Fred Hoyle has a recent version of the same. Karl Rahner sees in nature a power of self-transcendence grounded in the Absolute Being.

Rahner cautions, however, that we are not to think of the Creator as a demiurge, a fixer. A complete mechanism along with the technique for building a house does not take the place of a planner and builder, but it is no credit to the builder to say that the mechanism is incomplete and must be filled in by direct intervention. That is the solution of creationism, and it was the solution of a simpler age, animism, which supposed a spirit to make the tree grow and another to move the sun in its path. The Greeks propelled the West to an understanding of all reality at appropriate levels, and the task continues. We make no concession to materialistic reductionism or monism when we

84

search for a satisfactory mechanism for evolution, just as we do not belittle the builder when we study the process he uses. Conversely, openness to higher causes does not justify inserting them as a stopgap. These considerations guide us away from the pitfalls of both creationism and exaggerated evolutionism.

Summarizing to this point, we may say that in the late twentieth century we have before us adequate evidence that the universe and earth have been developing over billions of years, and that life on earth began some two billion years ago and became increasingly complex and varied. Many species are extinct while others appear late in the fossil record. The clean and simple theory is that all forms of life are related by common descent, and while this is not directly demonstrable, there is no compelling reason to think that it is not the order of nature, and so this part of the theory is also highly probable. The Neo-Darwinian causal chain of variation, natural selection, and isolation is demonstrably operative in nature, but considerable controversy remains as to its role in the evolutionary process.

A serious and persistent criticism of evolutionary theory starts from the improbability that random and mostly damaging mutations can account for evolutionary "improvements," so we need to give more attention to the question of chance and design.

5

Chance and Design

When we think of chance, we think of an unplanned occurrence. Luck may be something we want or do not want, but not something we can arrange. So at first sight chance and design or plan seem to be mutually exclusive. But on closer inspection we find that the two are mixed in real life. If we approach a crossing just too late to beat a long slow freight train, that is bad luck. But if we saw the train in time and chose not to race it, then our wait was planned. And of course the train arrived according to plan.

Since evolution is supposed to depend on chance events and creation on design, we can expect that the two sides in the controversy will be at loggerheads on this issue also. Extreme evolutionists are prone to make sweeping statements that the world "just happened," and that we came into existence entirely by chance. Reductionists relying on the indeterminacy encountered in modern atomic theory may be found saying that chance is the cause of everything, while Einstein protests that God does not play at dice.

On the other side creationists erect an impenetrable wall between chance and design. They argue through pages of figures against the probability that organic systems could have arisen by chance. What is the probability that four hundred amino acids will join by chance to form the particular sequence found in some vital protein? Since there are about twenty amino acids available, it will be one chance in 20^{400}, or one in 10^{520}. Not even billions of years would help much in arriving at just one protein molecule. Creationists quote the Russian biochemist Alexander Oparin, pioneer of the idea that life formed from a primordial soup, as saying that the probability that it happened by chance is about the same as the probability that a volcano would spew out a completely equipped factory. Therefore organisms came into existence by design, not by chance.

It would seem that the reasoning on both sides leaves too much to chance. The calculation of odds, beginning back in the days of Pascal and Fermat and developing into the mathematics of probability and statistics, is a vast subject important in both theory and commercial application. But it all starts with odds. The chance of seeing heads on a coin with one throw is one in two. The chance of throwing heads twice in succession is $1/2 \times 1/2$, or $1/4$, and so on. The chance that the coin will land on one side or the other is one, or mathematical certainty.

Whether heads or tails comes out on top is a matter of chance, but the chance can operate only within the limits of cause and effect. Going back to the classical four causes, we see that the first cause required is the form, the design. The coin must be effectively two-sided so it will not stand on edge, and not be biased like loaded dice. If the coin is melted down to a blob of metal there will no longer be any chance of throwing heads or tails. Secondly, the material must hold its shape. Warm butter will not do. Thirdly, the coin must be tossed by some efficient cause for chance to operate. When the coin is at rest the position is fixed and the chance of seeing the opposite side is zero until the coin is lifted again. To complete the four causes, there is the final cause, the purpose and direction behind every design, even those yielding chance. The cubic die is designed to provide a certain kind of odds and no other.

Like the protein example, games can yield impressive calculations. There are 52! (52x51x50...x1) ways of arranging 52 cards in a deck, so in shuffling there is one chance in 52! or 8×10^{67} that a particular arrangement will occur. All the four billion people now living could shuffle continuously for 6×10^{50} years, which is about 10^{40} times the estimated age of the universe, and still have only an even chance of turning up any particular arrangement, say the original order in which cards came from the factory. Still the cards are designed so that one of the 8×10^{67} arrangements is sure to come up with each shuffle. The order existing after the previous shuffle and the movement of the shuffler control the next arrangement physically, factors which the card shark would like to influence and remove from the realm of pure chance. After each shuffle the arrangement is fixed, no longer indeterminate, until the next shuffle begins. If the cards are burned to ashes, the chance of getting any card arrangement is reduced to zero. The chance of dealing one perfect hand, say all the spades, to one player, is one in 6×10^{11}, while the chance of dealing a single suit to each of the four players is one in 5×10^{28}. But a less than perfect hand is not fatal. Players do their thing with what they get, sometimes winning, sometimes losing.

• Chance in Evolution

In speaking of evolution, therefore, it does not make sense to consider chance and design as mutually exclusive. Appropriate design is always presupposed in chance. The element of chance, or lack of control or predictability by the human operator, may be present, but only within the limits of design. As Max Born says, "Nature is ruled by laws of cause and laws of chance in a certain mixture" (p. 3). On the purely physical plane even the fall of a coin is under the control of physical laws, but it is unwarranted to extend that kind of physical determinism to the whole human operation of tossing a coin. At its own level the chance mode of operation is real.

In applying the ideas about chance to the formation of organisms we must first correct an erroneous impression underlying the calculations of creationists and some evolutionists, namely, that proteins are formed by the fortuitous joining of amino acids as though they were dealt from a stack of cards or tossed into a box. Proteins are formed on a template on which each amino acid must fall into place, and the pattern is stored permanently in the DNA molecule. Biologist Theodosius Dobzhansky says that "not even mutations are random changes, because what mutations can take place in a given gene is evidently decreed by the structure of that gene" (Deely, p. 100). DNA is not shuffled like a deck of cards, but there is an occasional random alteration at some point on the long helical molecule. It is random because the fact and the time and the place of the encounter, no matter whether determinate or indeterminate on the part of the gamma ray or other source, were

89

not determined by the design of the DNA molecule. But the randomness is hemmed in on all sides by design, and while the organism, like the card player, can get by with a genetic heritage that is less than perfect, there are limits. Decades of forced mutation of the fruit fly *Drosophila* produced monstrous fruit flies but still fruit flies. Larger mutations were incompatible with the organism and produced no viable offspring.

We cannot imagine that it was any other way at any point in the long developmental process. If we start with the mythical "Big Bang" of modern astronomical theory, we suppose that the ylem (the primordial first substance) that exploded must have had a structure designed to explode. Everywhere we find the electromagnetic field with its marvelously ordered properties, the electrical and magnetic fields at right angles to each other and to the direction of propagation of radiation according to the right-hand rule of the electricians. Was a left-hand rule equally probable? Was it a matter of heads or tails? Is it due to something like the toss of a coin that the world is not made of antimatter, with heavy particles negatively charged and surrounded by positrons? If the chemical elements were formed by random collisions of more elementary particles, those particles were designed to join together in certain ways. If the elements combined to form cell-like, self-reproducing structures in the primordial ooze, they were following the chemical affinities designed into them, and the cell-like structures were fixed take-off points for further random modifications as the life processes went on. Still we find signs of fortuitous selection. The most abundant of all organic substances, D-glucose, or dextrose, is, as the name implies, of right-handed asymmetry in rotating polarized light. Did it win out over left-handed asymmetry by the toss of a coin? The highly improbable structure of DNA

90

makes one wonder how many other possible viable combinations were bypassed and overwhelmed when this one became dominant.

The element of chance continues in the scattering of seeds and the mating of animals and human couples, and this mixing of genes is more important in genetic variation than DNA mutation. Our parents probably met by chance, and our very existence and consciousness as individuals are contingent on that meeting. Would we exist if they had met someone else? We rightly call the meeting providential even though it was accidental, and that holds for all the chances that preceded it. From beginning to end in the development process there is no sign that events are out of control. They are simply allowed to proceed according to natural laws and the degree of determinacy or indeterminacy designed into them.

Chance, therefore, is an integral part of natural processes, the ones we see every day as well as those which reach back into the evolutionary time scale. It is absurd, however, to attribute everything to pure chance divorced from causality. W.R. Thompson puts it well: "If it were possible to construct a theory of evolution representing this process as due to pure chance, antifinalists might have some cause for satisfaction and finalists some cause for alarm. It will, however, be evident from what has already been said that a Universe of pure chance is, in the strict sense of the word, unthinkable, by which we mean, not simply something distasteful or dissatisfying, but something on which the mind cannot take hold at all. A world of pure chance is simply chaos, or absolute disorder, and the concept of absolute disorder has no positive intelligible content. Chance or fortuity is a by-product of finality. The fact that a certain event, or collection of events, is due to chance, therefore, does not annihilate the doctrine that fi-

91

nality exists in the Universe; without the assumption of finality the proposition could not even be stated" (Fothergill, p. 309).

Darwin also, in *The Descent of Man* (p. 378), recoils from the implications of blind chance: "I am aware that the conclusions arrived at in this work will be denounced by some as highly irreligious; but he who thus denounces them is bound to show why it is more irreligious to explain the origin of man as a distinct species by descent from some lower form, through the laws of variation and natural selection, than to explain the birth of the individual through laws of ordinary reproduction. The birth both of the species and of the individual are equally parts of that grand sequence of events, which our minds refuse to accept as the results of blind chance. The understanding revolts at such a conclusion, whether or not we are able to believe that every slight variation of structure, the union of each pair in marriage, the dissemination of each seed, and other events, have all been ordained for some special purpose."

Chance is an elusive concept. The human mind knows in terms of forms that transcend change. Chance focuses on change as indeterminate, as without pattern, and so it is unknowable almost by definition. We can deal with it only in terms of the causes surrounding it and of the probability patterns found in large numbers, namely, in terms of the laws of probability.

The subject is especially intractable for those who, like creationists and extreme evolutionists, set too wide a gap between chance and design. The creationists' calculations are really a waste of time and paper, since they assume incorrectly that complex living structures in the evolutionary scheme are supposed to have arisen by tossing simpler components into a pot, whereas, as we have seen, a preliminary structure is always at hand, much as an existing structure and pattern are always on hand to guide the more rapid development of an individual from seed to adult. Only the mutations are subject to chance. Even evolutionist Jacques Monod, in *Chance and Necessity*, while clinging to his anti-creation ideology and maintaining that man emerged only by chance, manages, at the cost of much labor and some inconsistency, to discover at least a part of what is obvious, namely, that there is some design within which chance operates, especially in the directedness of objects and in the irreversible pattern that emerges once the chance operation is completed.

More astonishing is the recent effort of the "non-Christian" Fred Hoyle, in *The Intelligent Universe*. His thesis is that life is a phenomenon of the universe, not just the earth, and that gene structures must have floated in from space. He supports it by repeating the arguments of the creationists against the probability that life could have arisen by chance from a primordial soup. It has about the same probability, he says, as that of a tornado ripping through an airplane junkyard and putting together an airplane ready to fly. His argument still shortchanges intermediate design and structure and so he is no more convincing than the creationists.

But he has a further thesis, namely, that a super intellect within the universe frees the process from the vagaries of chance. He tells us: "The intelligence responsible for the creation of carbon-based life in the cosmic theory is firmly within the Universe and is subservient to it. Because the creator of carbon-based life was not all-powerful, there is consequently no paradox in the fact that terrestrial life is far from ideal" (p. 236).

Thus in one fell swoop Hoyle wishes back on us the Hellenistic world mind, pantheism, and even more ancient animism, while echoing the objection of Lucretius and Darwin that God could not have created the world because there is too much wrong with it.

• Indeterminacy Theory

Another concept of chance which continues to intrude on the periphery of the subject of evolution is the indeterminacy aspect of quantum theory. The middle 1920s saw one of the greatest achievements in the history of science, matching Einstein's relativity theory of a few years earlier. It was the development of a theoretical model of the atom which accurately tied together and reproduced the experimental data, especially the energy levels of the spectrum. Acting on the idea of Louis de Broglie that the electron is associated with a wave, Irwin Schroedinger came up with a wave mechanics. At the same time Bohr's Copenhagan school developed a probability mechanics which proved equivalent to the wave mechanics.

At the heart of the probability quantum theory is Heisenberg's indeterminacy relationship, which states that the uncertainty of position in a subatomic particle times the uncertainty of its momentum can never be less than Planck's constant. There can be no doubt about the validity of this relationship in subatomic theory and calculation. The transistor, along with the computer and communication technologies built upon it, pays tribute to its correctness.

Nevertheless it has raised a few philosophical problems. To the end of his days Einstein could not agree that indeterminacy was at the bottom of things. God does not play at dice, is his famous objection. But Einstein was brought up on nineteenth-century determinism. We have seen that from our worm's eye vantage point God *does* seem to play at dice at times in his creation and providence, even in selecting our parents for us. We assume an adequate causality at some level, but it may not be accessible to us.

Indeterminacy also has a problematic philosophical background, expressed in the very terms used. Heisenberg called his famous relation indeterminacy (*Unbestimmtheit*), but he illustrates it by showing that any signal with a short enough wavelength to interact with an electron and reveal its position would have enough energy to kick it somewhere else. In other words, there is no physical means of knowing the position and momentum at the same time. The philosophical climate in scientific circles since Ernst Mach was positivistic: only observable pointer readings have meaning. In this climate the distinction between indeterminacy in the object and uncertainty (*Unsicherheit*) in knowing becomes blurred. English texts usually speak of the Uncertainty Principle, and while it is a mistranslation of the German, it is probably not a gross mistranslation of Heisenberg's meaning. So if we now ask whether the parameters of subatomic particles are indeterminate in themselves or merely unknowable, we find that quantum theory gives us an uncertain pointer reading. In any case we hold that any degree of indeterminacy in the objective subatomic world was designed into it. It did not get there by chance.

Chance is real; something about nature is free as a bird in flight, as unpredictable as the wind. Behind it is design and proper causality, but to reduce it to mechanical determinism is to miss it. It would be like explaining a symphony as the molecular motion of gases.

• Levels of Understanding

In some way a musical performance can be represented in terms of the molecular motion of gases. But there are various levels of human understanding, mutually compatible levels of theory, of explanatory systems and concepts, some more significant than others but all possibly contributing to overall knowledge. Music as gas movement would be an extreme case of mechanistic reductionism.

Another example: imagine that you heard disturbing noises in your car engine. You could consult a garage mechanic or an engineer. The garage man may have failed mathematics but understands everything about engines. He may tell you what you need before you ask. Only rarely will he have to consult an automotive engineer. The engineer can give you an elegant theory but he may be slow finding the noisy water pump on your model. The two men have complete knowledge of the same object at different levels, both significant and each compatible with the other.

Darwinism and Neo-Darwinism approach the origin of things at the level of biological and chemical process. They offer a plausible cause-effect mechanism at this level in theories of genetic variation and natural selection. But other thinkers have not only found the theory incomplete at its own mechanical level but have pointed out that the mechanical level is not the only one or even the most important one. Their hard task has been to show that a different approach can add significant understanding in the face of the reductionist mentality of evolutionism. Catholics have been involved in this effort, and a survey of the Catholic response to Darwinism is in order here.

6

The Catholic Response to Evolution

• The First Vatican Council

The First Vatican Council met in 1869-1870, ten years after the publication of Darwin's *Origin of Species*, the first general council since Trent in the sixteenth century and therefore the first to address itself to a world that had grown up with modern science. Evolutionary theory confronts the Church with the need for clarification in three broad areas: (1) the doctrines of Creation, the Fall, and Redemption; (2) the interpretation of Scripture; and (3) the relation between revelation and natural knowledge, between faith and science. The following points made at the Council, while addressing the more general situation, are relevant to evolution (Denzinger, 1782-1799):

1. Against any exaggerated evolutionary notion that the world "just happened," the Council reaffirms the first article of the Creed, professing Catholic faith in the "one God . . . Creator of heaven and earth . . . essentially distinct from the world."

2. Rejecting deism with its notion of a Creator who wound up the world and then looked on from a distance, the Council professes that "by his providence he protects and governs everything he has made."

3. The Council makes it a dogma of faith that the Creator can be known with certainty by reason: "If anyone says that the one and true God, our Creator and Lord, cannot be known with certainty from what he has made by the natural light of human reason, let him be anathema" (Denzinger, 1806).

4. The revelation necessary for man's supernatural destiny is contained in tradition and in the canonical books of Scripture which, "inspired by the Holy Spirit have God as their Author" and have been "committed to the Church" whose prerogative it is "to pass judgment on the true meaning and interpretation of Sacred Scripture." Thus the Council asserts the Catholic position in the face of the destructive rationalistic exegesis of the time as well as against the Protestant belief in private interpretation and Scripture as the sole rule of faith. Catholic fundamentalists need to ask whether their interpretation of Scripture is that of the Catholic Church.

5. The Council states that while there are sure signs

that God has spoken, faith itself is a divine gift. It goes on: "All those things are to be believed with divine and Catholic faith which are contained in God's word, written or handed down by tradition, and which are proposed for belief as divinely revealed by either the solemn judgment or the ordinary and universal teaching of the Church."

We note, therefore, that looking up the ancient sources is only a start. What is to be believed must be faithful to the record *and* taught by the living Church.

6. The Council teaches that faith and reason are distinct sources of knowledge, but that they cannot oppose each other, since God is the source of both. Opinions, therefore, which are clearly contrary to faith may not be defended as "legitimate conclusions of science."

7. Both faith and the human sciences should be free to move forward following their own principles and methods. They can be mutually helpful.

• Pope Leo XIII

The Scripture question was taken up again in 1893 in Pope Leo XIII's encyclical *Providentissimus Deus*, which provides some guidelines for interpreting the Genesis story of creation.

The pope encouraged the scientific study of Scripture to counteract the rationalists who were trying to reduce it to "stupid fables and lying stories." These rationalists, he said, are the true heirs of the older heretics who, "repudiating the divine traditions and the teaching office of the Church, held the Scriptures to be the one source of revelation and the final appeal in matters of faith" (No. 10). "The Holy Fathers, we say, are of supreme authority whenever they all interpret in one and the same manner any text of the Bible, as pertaining to the doctrine of faith or morals; for their unanimity clearly evinces that such interpretation has come down to us from the Apostles as a matter of Catholic faith" (No. 14).

Concerning natural science Pope Leo said: "There can never be any real discrepancy between the theologian and the physicist, as long as each confines himself within his own lines, and both are careful, as St. Augustine warns, 'not to make rash assertions, or to assert what is not known as known.' "

What can be really demonstrated as true in science "we must show to be capable of reconciliation with our Scriptures." The sacred writers and the Holy Spirit who spoke through them did not intend to teach what was not profitable to salvation or seek to penetrate the secrets of nature; rather, they dealt with these things in figurative language or in terms in common use at the time (No. 18). The Fathers also expressed the ideas of their own times, and "thus made statements which in these days have been abandoned as incorrect." Hence we must carefully note what they say belongs to faith and what they are unanimous in. For the rest we are "at liberty to hold divergent opinions." On the other hand much that natural science has held was afterward rejected (No. 19).

"It is absolutely wrong . . . to narrow inspiration to certain parts of Holy Scripture, or to admit that the sacred writer erred." For all the canonical books "are written wholly and entirely, with all their parts, at the dictation of the Holy Spirit." Inspired writers were his instruments, and we cannot say that "perhaps the instruments fell into error." For what the Holy Spirit inspired them to write "they first rightly understood, then willed faithfully to write down, and finally expressed in apt words and infallible truth" (No. 20).

This concept of total inspiration, expressed aptly but in popular language, was to be the key to Catholic under-

100

standing of Genesis as evolution emerged. In those early years, the second half of the nineteenth century, there was rapid progress along with storm and stress at the interface of natural science and revelation.

• Concordism

In 1870 the Reverend Gerald Molloy, professor of theology at St. Patrick's College, Maynooth, Ireland, wrote *Geology and Revelation*, in which he applied the "popular language" idea to the conflict between the heliocentric system and the passage in the Book of Joshua which says that the sun stood still. "Learned men once believed that the Book of Joshua represented the succession of day and night as produced by the revolution of the sun around the earth, whereas it is now considered quite plain that the Book of Joshua, properly understood, teaches nothing of the kind; but that the Inspired Writer, in describing a wonderful phenomenon of Nature, simply employs the language of men according to the established usage of his time" (p. 27).

In dealing, however, with the six days of creation the Reverend Gerald Molloy is not quite ready for the same step. He proposes two hypotheses. The first is that God "created" (*bara*, in Hebrew) the world long eons before the first biblical day, and then "formed" it in six days. The second hypothesis is that the "day" (*yōm*) is a period of indefinite length, flexible enough to accommodate the geological periods. The second hypothesis is known as "concordism" (that is, trying to translate the Bible so it means what science means); it was well received in the early years and is still found among some creationists. It soon became evident, however, that this was not the way to go. It changes the meaning of the words to something the sacred author could not have known without special revelation, a meaning without religious purpose, without prece-

101

dent, and without support in tradition. The right way is not to look for a new meaning but to try to get closer to the original meaning of the sacred author.

• Mivart

St. George Jackson Mivart was a Catholic scientist who started on the ground floor of evolution and worked to harmonize it with religious belief. He became a Catholic during the Oxford Movement in 1843 (Gruber, p. 15). He made a name for himself as a biologist and at first accepted Darwin's theory. But he soon found it too materialistic and mechanistic and argued that there must be divine guidance behind it, much to the chagrin of his old friends Darwin and Huxley. Darwin enlarged the sixth edition of *The Origin of Species* to respond to Mivart's criticism. Mivart describes his work as follows: "In my book on the *Genesis of Species* I had in view two main objects. My first was to show that the Darwinian theory is untenable, and that 'Natural Selection' is not the origin of species. My second was to demonstrate that nothing even in Mr. Darwin's theory (as put forth before the publication of his *Descent of Man*) and, a fortiori, nothing in Evolution generally, was necessarily antagonistic to Christianity" (1876, p. 429).

What interests us particularly is that after writing *Genesis of Species* to show that evolution is not antagonistic to Christianity, Mivart was honored with a doctorate in philosophy by Pope Pius IX. The Church was already saying that the problem was not evolution, or transformism, but rather the evolutionists' materialism and disregard for the special nature of man.

Mivart dedicated his 1876 work, *Lessons from Nature*, to John Henry Newman, who had previously written to him regarding his *Genesis of Species*: "It is pleasant to find that the first real exposition of the logical insufficiency of

Mr. Darwin's theory comes from a Catholic. In saying this, you must not suppose that I have personally any great dislike or dread of his theory, but a good many people are much troubled at it" (Vol. 25, p. 446).

Mivart's later speculations led him astray. He tried to soften the harshness of the doctrine of damnation in his book *Happiness in Hell*, which went on the Index of Forbidden Books. Further aberrations appeared in his writings, and when Archbishop Herbert Vaughan sent him a list of errors to retract, he refused and was excommunicated in 1900. Mivart was perhaps somewhat deranged from his final illness, and he died a few months later.

• Schell

In Germany Herman Schell (1850-1906), "the most significant Roman Catholic dogmatician of the last century" (Kaiser), wrote a penetrating assessment of Darwinian evolution as an integral part of his overall theology of a dynamic triune God. His works also spent some time on the Index in an era when the Roman congregations were very cautious because of the real menace of modernism, which tended, with varying degrees of rashness, to change essential Catholic teaching to fit the evolving times.

Father Schell saw all of reality as directed toward progress, and he easily accepted the idea of evolution itself. But he found Darwin's theory of natural selection inadequate. At the scientific level he pointed out the limitations of chance and insisted that the empirically learned relationships in nature point to a plan. Plan and development can be explained only by a spiritual order. At the biological level, he went on, if the whole is greater than the sum of its parts, or if the whole has life and sensation and consciousness when the parts do not, then the whole must be a reality capable of making use of the parts for its own advantage and not merely be subject to mechanical selection and elimination at a lower level. This emphasis on wholeness is a recurring theme which continues to this day to challenge the reductionist orthodoxy of Neo-Darwinism.

• Teilhard de Chardin

The most famous as well as most controversial Catholic writer on evolution is the French Jesuit Pierre Teilhard de Chardin (1881-1955). Enthusiasts may hail him as the greatest thinker of the century, while his detractors call him a heretic or a fraud or both. Evolutionist Julian Huxley wrote an introduction to Teilhard's *The Phenomenon of Man* and approved its focus on man, but of course stopped short of its focus on God as the Omega Point; Sir Peter Medawar, on the other hand, called his ideas "pious bunk" (Clark, p. 325). Teilhard is even accused of having been involved in planting the "Piltdown man," a fairly recent skull with human teeth found with the lower jaw of an ape on which the teeth had been carefully filed to match the upper jaw. The trick fooled the experts for forty years, until 1953, after which Teilhard shared with Dawson, the man with whom he shared the discovery, the suspicion of being a perpetrator of the hoax (Ruse, p. 239; Johanson, p. 52). Sir Arthur Conan Doyle, creator of Sherlock Holmes, has also been accused, and this indicates perhaps how circumstantial and flimsy the evidence is. (For Teilhard's defense, see Thomas King's *Teilhard and the Unity of Knowledge*.)

In his efforts to treat evolution both scientifically and theologically, Teilhard may be compared to a noted physics professor several decades ago. When physicists heard him lecture they thought he was a good philosopher, and when philosophers heard him they thought he was a good physicist. Teilhard was trained in a scholasticism which went past him for the most part, and in geology-paleontology, but he soared beyond the foundation provided by any science. His intuition "saw" the universal law of increasing complexity driven by a "radial energy" built into nature, evolving inevitably into human consciousness, and into human society converging toward an eventual unity in the Omega Point, the end of creation, which he identified with Christ.

A positive contribution is his enthusiastic poetic insight creating a synthesis of organic evolution with the upward movement of history that has been an essential mark of Judeo-Christianity since the call of Abraham. A weakness is that he views that movement as part of the natural sweep of things, so that original sin and redemption are an uneasy fit, and faith in the supernatural intervention of God in the Incarnation is therefore threatened with atrophy. His works were published in the late 1950s, and in 1962 the Holy Office issued a *monitum*, an exhortation to those in charge of education to beware of the "dangers presented by the works of Fr. Teilhard and his followers," which "abound in such ambiguities, and indeed even serious errors, as to offend Catholic doctrine" (Sennot, p. 51). On the other hand a letter from the papal secretary of state on the occasion of the centennial of his birth stressed the great value of his contribution (Frye, p. 78).

Norbert Luyten, O.P., draws this conclusion: "While appreciating the effort involved with its bold sweep, one cannot overlook the internal weakness of the synthesis. A 'physics of the spirit' remains a very questionable enterprise. It is much to be feared that it will lead only to confusion of essential differences" (p. 12).

• Messenger
Pope Leo XIII had declared that the unanimous teaching of the Fathers in interpreting Scripture on a matter of

doctrine was a final authority. During the relatively quiet interval between the two World Wars the Reverend Ernest Messenger, in *Evolution and Theology*, dispelled any notion that the Fathers of the Church were unanimous in interpreting Genesis or in teaching the manner in which creation took place.

The Fathers of the allegorical school of Alexandria taught that everything was created simultaneously, not over a period of six days, and we have seen that Saint Augustine was of the same mind. Saint Gregory of Nyssa expressed his understanding of simultaneous creation in these words: "the necessary arrangement of nature required succession in the things coming into being," but there was only "one motion of the divine will."

Genesis does not say simply, as creationists do, that God created plants and animals according to their kinds, but rather "let the earth bring forth," and "let the waters bring forth" these things, and only then follow the words, "and so God made. . . ." The Fathers taught in similar terms. Saint Ephrem says, "The earth then produced everything with the aid of the waters and the light." Saint Basil thought mud was still producing eels, and that birds came from water. Saint John Chrysostom attributes vital activity to water, and Saint Ambrose said that the earth generates plants. Chrysostom warns against trying to understand everything, since we cannot even understand how bread becomes blood and bile. We have seen how Augustine labored to find a satisfactory understanding of the first chapters of Genesis. Pope Pius XII, in *Divino Afflante Spiritu*, concludes that the Fathers found those chapters "well nigh unintelligible" and that we should go beyond Christian antiquity but in a way harmonious with the general current of tradition.

Saints in the Middle Ages, including Bonaventure, Albert, and Thomas Aquinas, followed the old Greek view, already witnessed to by Cosmas Indicopleustes, that the heavenly bodies were moved by spirits, and Aquinas and Albert thought that the active power of bringing forth living things came from heavenly bodies.

The early Church of course had no inkling of the evolutionary theories that would emerge from the modern scientific revolution, but the opponents of evolution, no matter what other reasons they may have, cannot appeal to the constant teaching of the Church that the world was created in six days and that biological species were created separately. The Fathers are unanimous on the fact of creation, but not on the way it happened.

• Pope Pius XII

In 1943, following the lead of Leo XIII in *Providentissimus Deus*, Pope Pius XII wrote the encyclical *Divino Afflante Spiritu* to encourage biblical scholarship. Among the guidelines given there we may stress the following as applicable to Genesis:

1. To read intelligently we should know the literary forms used by the biblical writers in recording the facts and events of history (No. 79). Saint Athanasius had already pointed out the need to know the occasions and the purpose of the writing.

2. The sacred writer speaks of the physical order "by what appears to the senses" (No. 65). The Holy Spirit did not intend to teach things unprofitable to salvation, such as the essential nature of visible things (No. 66). It is not an error to use ordinary speech (No. 80). The words of God expressed in human language are made like human speech in every respect except error (No. 79).

3. There is no completely satisfactory solution to all problems (No. 82). The definitions of the Church are few,

and skill is to be freely exercised (No. 83). The efforts of laborers in the field are to be judged "not only with equity and justice but also with the greatest charity. All should abhor the intemperate zeal which imagines that whatever is new should for that reason be opposed or suspect" (No. 47).

In 1949, on the eve of *Humani Generis*, William H. McClellan, S.J., of St. Mary's, Woodstock, Maryland, summarized the Catholic position on evolution in this way: "Briefly, evolution of non-human organic species offers no point of opposition to Catholic belief, so long as a Supreme Intelligence is admitted as the first cause. Mankind forms an exception, as by every right it should. No evolutionary process can account for a rational soul. Of the first human body such an origin is possible without prejudice to faith, but not to be held as positively probable until solid evidence is at hand. This is, in broad lines, the unchanged status of the question for Catholics" (Messenger, 1949, p. 76).

Then in 1950, nearly a century after Darwin had published *The Origin of Species*, Pope Pius XII became the first pope to deal with evolution officially as part of the encyclical *Humani Generis*. It was anything but an enthusiastic endorsement of the modern theory, but it was a clear directive to study it openly with certain precautions to safeguard religion and Catholic teaching. Here are some relevant points of the encyclical:

1. Beware the monistic and pantheistic opinion that the world is in continual evolution (No. 5). Communists love that kind of evolution.

2. Do not abandon the traditional philosophy "which safeguards the genuine validity of human knowledge, the unshakable metaphysical principles of sufficient reason, causality, and finality, and finally the mind's ability to attain certain and unchangeable truth" (No. 29).

108

3. The Church does not forbid discussion by those experienced in both theology and science of the evolution of the human body. Catholic faith obliges us to hold that souls are immediately created by God. Some rashly speak as if the origin of the human body from preexisting matter were already proved, as though the sources of divine revelation did not require the "greatest moderation and caution" on this question (No. 36).

4. On another conjectural opinion — namely, polygenism — there is less liberty. "For the faithful cannot embrace that opinion which maintains either that after Adam there existed on this earth true men who did not take their origin through natural generation from him as from the first parent of all or that Adam represents a certain number of first parents" (No. 37).

5. The first eleven chapters of Genesis "pertain to history in the true sense" even though they do not conform to the methods of Greco-Roman or modern historians. Guided by divine inspiration they use simple and metaphorical language adapted to a simple people to state the principal truths of salvation and to "give a popular description of the origin of the human race and the chosen people" (No. 38). These narratives are not "myths" (No. 39).

This encyclical, with its provisional stance, remains the principal statement of the magisterium on evolution. After 1950, Catholic scholars speculated more freely on evolution, taking positions ranging from total rejection to enthusiastic acceptance, the median position being some kind of theistic evolution. Thumbnail notes on a few of the leading contributors may help to clarify the Catholic view.

• Ruffini

The highest-ranking churchman to enter the lists was Ernesto Cardinal Ruffini in 1959 with *The Theory of Evolu-*

tion Judged by Reason and Faith. At the theological level he sees room for diversity of opinion. The historical content of Genesis is that God created the universe in time, something that cannot be demonstrated clearly by reason. The enumeration of the seven days is given for religious reasons, and having God work at creation is pure anthropomorphism (that is, it imagines God as acting the way a human being would). He holds that Adam was created from nothing and Eve from Adam, even though Cajetan held a contrary opinion. At the level of science he accepts the long ages indicated by the measured distances of the galaxies, and the long temporal sequence of living species, but argues that succession in time does not show genetic succession or evolution, which still remains unproved.

• Nogar

In *The Wisdom of Evolution*, Raymond Nogar, O.P., reviews the scientific evidence for the factual aspect of evolution and says that it is enough to satisfy reasonable doubt even though it is circumstantial. He distinguishes evolution as hypothesis, theory, and fact, from evolution as ideology as it is found in Julian Huxley and Teilhard de Chardin. While evolution is highly probable as a fact of nature, it is an incomplete account of man, and the term becomes equivocal when applied to social progress.

At the theological level he says that the Bible is silent on evolution. Selecting an appropriate and probable scenario for the creation of Adam and Eve is problematic. Does Eve coming from Adam simply mean that they have the same nature? Was Adam perhaps the embryo of a near-human creature? Was he physically primitive but endowed with preternatural gifts? Such schemes are hybrids from revelation on the one hand and archaeology on the other, and verification is probably beyond the reach of scientific evidence.

110

Nogar provides valuable philosophical reflections on all aspects of evolution. For him the evolutionary plan points most convincingly to a divine Designer.

• Rahner

Coming from the scholastic tradition as well as modern thought in all areas of theology, Karl Rahner, S.J., contributed also to the doctrine of creation in its confrontation with evolution. Two thoughts from his *Hominization* should be useful here.

1. The Book of Genesis should be read as historical etiology (or the study of causes in history). Ancient peoples were accustomed to explain their present existence and condition by telling a story about what happened in the past. This is mythical etiology, since for the most part the story was a myth, a tale about something that never happened, like the myth of Sisyphus pushing a rock up a hill, although it embodied a profound truth about the people. Genesis should be considered historical etiology, showing the meaning and the "roots" of the chosen people, not in imaginary legends and myths but in the narrative of real events, events which are recalled, however, not as by eyewitnesses in the remote cases but as the recollections of the people told in popular narrative form. "If the account is read in some other way than this, it is not being taken more literally and seriously, but is being misunderstood" (p. 42).

2. The second thought is expressed succinctly: "God is not a demiurge." This expression takes into account the mystery of absolute divine trancendence standing against the fact that nothing in the universe can exist without God's immediate activity in creation, preservation, concurrence, and physical premotion. He is the First Cause making secondary causes possible and acting through them,

yet he does not work in tandem with them, at the same level. Like Augustine, Rahner finds that piecemeal creation in the creationist mold would reduce God, having him work at the level of the secondary deities imagined by ancient Gnosticism, the demiurges who were supposed to have created the world.

• Mynarek

An imposing study of evolution from the Catholic viewpoint is *Der Mensch, Sinnziel der Weltentwicklung (Man, the Goal of World Evolution)*, by the Reverend Hubertus Mynarek. With Teutonic thoroughness he investigates the whole field, in 393 dense pages of text and 116 pages of references and notes, 1,499 endnotes in all.

Mynarek takes as his starting point the work of Herman Schell, and thus establishes a continuity in Catholic thought over nearly a century. In broad outlines the conclusions of the two theologians are the same: evolution of species and of inorganic nature is not opposed to theology, and the general theme of progress is quite Christian, but some aspects of the theory are unsatisfactory. In the words of Schell: "In the interest of proving God's existence there is no point in opposing the natural development of distinct species; we oppose only that evolutionary theory which admits only mechanical causes and assumes a development without thought or purpose but which nevertheless has led to the existing order through a chaotic play of chance" (pp. 70-71).

While insisting, however, that there is no conflict between theology and a properly delimited theory of evolution, Mynarek is at considerable pains to show, on the authority of thoughtful scientists and from internal considerations, that Neo-Darwinism is seriously deficient at its own level of scientific explanation.

112

• Recent Statements of the Church

In the *Pastoral Constitution on the Church in the Modern World* the Second Vatican Council recalled the statement of Vatican I that there are two autonomous sources of knowledge, faith and reason, and that there can be no real conflict between them. Modern conditions tend to purify religions of remnants of magic and superstition so that many are achieving a more vivid sense of God (No. 7). The independence of temporal affairs does not mean they can be used without reference to the Creator, "for without the Creator the creature would vanish" (No. 36).

The Council deplores habits of mind sometimes found among Christians "which do not sufficiently attend to the rightful independence of science." As the note to No. 36 (above) indicates, this was a deliberate reference to the condemnation of Galileo, and may be taken as an apology for the unfortunate and unwise action taken by Church agencies in the seventeenth century. Pope John Paul II, in an address to the Pontifical Academy of Sciences on November 10, 1979 (*Origins*, p. 391), goes further in making amends, praising Galileo for his admirable understanding of the relation between faith and science and his insight into the interpretation of Scripture.

In another speech to the scientific community on October 3, 1981, he speaks of the creation of the universe in this way: "Sacred Scripture wishes simply to declare that the world was created by God, and in order to teach this truth it expresses itself in terms of the cosmology in use at the time of the writer. . . . Any other teaching about the origin and makeup of the universe is alien to the intentions of the Bible, which does not wish to teach how heaven was made but how one goes to heaven" (*Origins*, p. 279).

This is an obvious reference to Galileo's famous saying (based on Augustine): "The Bible does not teach us how the heavens go, but how to go to heaven." One would have to be fairly dense not to see that it was the pope's intention to warn against repeating the mistake of the Galileo case by condemning the scientific theory of evolution on the basis of a faulty interpretation of the Bible.

After this, an occasional reference to evolution by the pope should raise no eyebrows. In April 1985 he had this to say at a symposium on evolution: "Rightly comprehended faith in creation or a correctly understood teaching of evolution does not create obstacles: Evolution in fact presupposes creation; creation situates itself in the light of evolution as an event which extends itself through time — as a continual creation — in which God becomes visible to the eyes of the believer as 'creator of heaven and earth' " (*National Catholic Register*, May 12, 1985).

On June 21, 1985, the Holy Father spoke to a group of scientists on stellar evolution, as was reported in the July 15, 1985, edition of *L'Osservatore Romano* (pp. 11-12):

> It is wonderful to see how much has been understood concerning the structure of stars — their birth, life and death, the origin and structure of galaxies, the formation of elements and other building blocks of physical reality in the early universe, and the interlocking roles of fundamental interaction and processes, in the large and in the small.
>
> These scientific achievements proclaim the dignity of the human being and greatly clarify man's unique role in the universe.

On January 29, 1986, the pope restated his view of evolution in a general audience: "Indeed, the theory of natural evolution, understood in a sense that does not exclude divine causality, is not in principle opposed to the truth about creation of the visible world, as presented in the Book of Genesis" (*The Wanderer*, February 20, 1986).

In this country the bishops of Louisiana, as a guide to their people during the creationism-in-schools controversy raging in their state, issued in 1983 a statement in much the same language we have already seen: Scripture does not teach science, and commentators of the past did not settle the issue of how Scripture is to be interpreted concerning the origin of things. The bishops conclude with this admonition: "Christians should not reduce biblical truths which are so rich and profoundly spiritual to the level of uncritical or simplistic literalism. This would rob the Scriptures of their genuine meaning and salvific power" (*Origins*, p. 603).

From all this it should be clear that six-day creationism is badly out of tune with the teaching Church, which has slowly and cautiously accepted the prevailing scientific ideas and language of evolution and become comfortable with it, just as it learned earlier to think in heliocentric terms and of a spherical earth. Prior to that time the Church never taught that the earth was flat or that the sun went around it, even though there were times when most churchmen thought so. Now it does not teach that the world evolved, or is round, or orbits the sun. That is not its commission. These easy references to scientific theories merely assure us that they are not in conflict with the faith.

7

Creation

For Catholics and all Christians the fundamental doctrine in all this is creation, which means that God is the Author of everything, producing all by his free and incomprehensible act. That God created everything in the universe is a statement that stands on its own solid base, unshaken, though not untouched, by evolution in its various aspects on the one hand and creationism on the other. The First Vatican Council tells us that the statement derives from reason, that the Creator can be known, and with certainty, from what he has made. The Council simply quotes Romans 1:20, echoing a still older passage from the Book of Wisdom (13:1-9) which rebukes those who do not recognize the craftsman from his works. The tradition of the knowability of God from his creation is an ancient one.

The Council Fathers did not tell us what learning process to follow to find God in nature, since the possibilities are very broad, but they were well acquainted with the five ways presented by Saint Thomas Aquinas (*Summa Theologica*, I, q. 2, a. 3). It will serve our purpose to bring them down from the shelf where they have been languishing lately and dust them off to see how they look in this age of evolution and creationism. We shall reverse the order of the five ways, since the first, from motion, which Aquinas found most evident, is least evident to us, and the fifth, the way from design, is, as Father Nogar says, the most evident from an evolving world.

• Design in Evolution

In the chapter on ideology we looked at what Cardinal Newman called "the logical insufficiency of Mr. Darwin's theory" and tried to show from the opinion of a wide spectrum of thinkers and from the elementary logic of the case that the Neo-Darwinian mechanism of variation, selection, and isolation is inadequate to account for upward evolution. It is an impressive analysis of the process, but the cause it assigns does not match the effect.

A second logical insufficiency lies in the attempt to substitute chance for design and purpose in nature. Nineteenth-century materialists eagerly embraced Darwin because they thought he had removed teleology, or purposive design, from biology and made it an "objective" science. He did not succeed in doing this. The very expression "struggle for existence" indicates that he saw that there was more involved in biological development than a random push from behind. Chance, as we saw, supposes design, and in this case a design that enables an organism to struggle for existence rather than float passively on its environment. In the opinion of Loren Eiseley, "The struggle for existence, the willingness of the organism to struggle, a fact which Darwin does not attempt to explain, equates at least partially, though perhaps not quite so teleologically, with Lamarck's life-power, or perfecting principle." A modern French source (*Science Digest*, January 1961) even speaks of the "good judgment" of the organism in controlling genetic change.

This kind of active selection is observable at all levels from atom to mind, with the integral unit in charge as the principal agent. It selects for its own advantage, its own good, and this fact pushes hard against a whole level of reality that the positivist and reductionist temper found in science likes to avoid: good, design, purpose, plan.

Purpose and finality are found everywhere as direction or tendency. Each molecule has a design which determines not only its inner nature but also how it reaches beyond itself, what it aims at. Its design enables a molecule to form crystals, and the design of the crystal enables it to select molecules for growth. A vegetable is designed to grow and propagate. Wings are designed for flying, and regardless of ideology biologists are always looking for the function and purpose designed into every part of an organism. Failure to find an immediate purpose — as, for example, in the case of the vestigial digits of a horse — often simply points to the larger design of evolution. Design is as real and as observable as a bird's wings.

The search for an evolutionary mechanism does underscore a common abuse of teleology. To the question "Why do birds have wings?" the answer "In order to fly" or "God gave them wings so they could fly" is a short circuit that harks back to animism, the belief that every tree contained a spirit to make it grow. Darwinian mechanism draws our attention to secondary causes at work through a long evolutionary process, and they complete our understanding of nature. Nevertheless, the finalistic answer is basic: wings serve a purpose, and they are designed for flying.

118

• Mind

We are now driven to a new level. Design is inconceivable without mind. Design is an active verb as well as a product. A human designer chooses his material with an understanding of its existing design, and the new design he imposes on the material is conceived in the ideal order before it takes shape in the material. That this connection between mind and design is found in nature becomes apparent from a simple consideration. In nature a material crystal cannot contain its own design before the crystal exists. The molecules which are about to form the crystal do not contain the design of the crystal in any actual way; they are not crystals. The capacity to link the two material objects, molecule and crystal, by a design or plan in the ideal order that transcends matter and time is called mind. We see no way out of this link between design and spiritual mind, even though we do not understand the complete process by which this spiritual order operates on matter. We do not understand, for example, how an architect's design proceeds to move the carpenter's hammer. But we see it happen and take for granted that there is a sufficient connection.

• The Fifth Way

On this foundation of experience with design Saint Thomas Aquinas erects the fifth of his famous five ways of learning that God exists. The wording of the article brings this out subtly but clearly: "The fifth way is taken from the government of things. For we see that things which lack knowledge, such as natural bodies, operate for an end. This is apparent from the fact that they always or most often operate in the same way in order to achieve what is best. Whence it is evident that they arrive at the end not by chance but by intention. But those things which do not

119

have knowledge do not tend toward an end unless directed by a knowing and intelligent someone, as an arrow by an archer. Therefore there is some intelligence by which all natural things are directed to an end; and this we call God."

Fred Hoyle used a similar argument against evolution by chance, veering off only from the last five words, "and this we call God," in favor of an immanent world intelligence. But an immanent world intelligence solves nothing. A designer is different from his product, stands outside it, and precedes it in the order of cause if not of time. He does not design himself from scratch.

Computer design suggests further exploration of this idea by opening up the far-out prospect of a machine that could improve itself by feedback and regenerative capacity. It might even build another machine which would continue to improve the design according to the model which evolutionists find in nature. But there is no way the machine can be thought of as designing itself. It was not there to do it.

The designer of a self-correcting machine has to be much more clever than a plodding one-at-a-time designer. Theistic evolutionists maintain that the design of an evolving universe which achieves perfection through natural, even random, processes, is a much greater tribute to the divine Designer than piecemeal creationism.

• The Fourth Way — The Metaphysical Level

The arguments for the existence of God as summarized by Saint Thomas Aquinas are wide-ranging, but they all suppose two things beyond positivism. One is that there is a sufficient reason for things in the real world. Bertrand Russell's dictum that the world "just happened" does not fit either the world he knew or the intelligence he used. The second is that reality is not limited to the material and sense-perceptible. If two apples are added to two apples, the addition is as real as the apples, even though the addition itself is not sense-perceptible or material. If the heart movement is the direct cause of the movement of the blood, the cause-and-effect relation is as real as the sense-perceptible movements of heart and blood. Realities like cause and effect which reach beyond time and matter and the physical are called metaphysical.

In his fourth way Aquinas points to those attributes of things which are quite real in our world and experience but which nevertheless look not only beyond matter but into infinity as their maximum, such as being, goodness, truth, life, beauty, and intelligence. By contrast, a quality like redness can exist in the real order only in a material object, and once the wavelength of red is decided upon, nothing can be more red than that. Goodness, on the other hand, which means the correspondence of a thing to its ideal, can be found in anything and extend as far as being itself, which has no limit. A material thing can be more or less good. Goodness is not included in its essential pattern or nature but looks to a source outside itself which is good by nature and which we call God. To most people transcendent attributes like goodness and beauty stand out very strikingly in nature and speak of God more eloquently than anything else.

• The Third Way — Contingent and Necessary Being
The third way of Saint Thomas Aquinas focuses on being itself, the central theme of creation and the primary transcendental reality that looks into infinity. Why are there beings and not just nothing? This is the perennial query of the philosophical mind. Everything we know is here today and gone tomorrow. Things in our experience

are contingent, dependent on something else, and they could just as well not be. Existence is not a necessary part of their nature. It belongs to the nature of a stone to have hardness, shape, mineral composition, but "to be" is not included. There was a time when it was not, even though its nature was found in other stones; so of its nature it can either be or not be. To exist it must look to a source outside of its nature, a source which does not suffer from this same shortcoming but whose nature includes existence. Such a source we call God.

Atheists sometimes respond to the contingency argument by saying that while individual items in the universe come and go, the whole universe exists necessarily. Of course we cannot witness the beginning or end of the whole universe as we witness the beginning and end of a garden plant, but neither can we find a reason why the whole universe should be any less contingent than the garden plant, why existence should be essential to its nature. It does not violate anything we know about this universe to suppose that it did not always exist or that it might cease to exist. The idea of a necessary changing universe involves an internal contradiction. It is not even good science fiction.

A scientist once remarked on a television program that science is ultimately searching for a law that will be necessary. It is an admission of the contingency of all known laws, and by extension, of nature's existence. The necessary law, or physical principle, which that scientist and others are hoping for would eliminate that contingency and include the necessary existence which we ascribe to God, making the Creator superfluous (Jaki, p. 86).

That hope is so foreign to the evidence of nature that it is more honest to proceed to the second response of the atheist to the question of why the universe exists: "It just

122

happened" or "It just is." This response upsets the whole scientific enterprise, which looks for the reasons for things. There is a saying that philosophy looks for the why and science looks for the how, but that saying merely adds confusion. All science searches for the why at its own level. The agnostic says the particular sciences cannot deal with the ultimate questions, and that is correct: they do not deal at that level. Then he denies that there is another valid approach or carefully avoids trying one.

It should be emphasized that the theist, the believer in a transcendent deity, does not know how God's nature makes his existence necessary. He has no privileged insight on this point, and in fact we insist that God's inner nature is basically inaccessible to the human mind probing from the outside. We judge from the nature we know that God must be, and that in some way he must have those attributes which will account for what is seen in creation, but it is a negative approach. His existence is not contingent like ours, and his goodness is not separable from his nature and imperfect as ours is. This is a confession of profound ignorance, but it steers clear of the irrational posture to which extreme evolutionism is driven: It just happened. The atheist says there is no reason for the existence of the world. The theist says there is, but that it is found in a source essentially different from the world we know, a source that exists by the necessity of its nature.

• The Second Way — Cause and Effect

Saint Thomas Aquinas derives the second way of knowing that God exists by considering efficient causality. Positivists in science appear to be following David Hume (see, for example, pp. 54, 74, and 77 of his *Enquiries*), who claimed that we know only the juxtaposition of phenomena, not that one is the cause of another. A gun discharges and a bullet flies out, and Hume will not allow us to be sure that the discharge caused the bullet to come out. Scientists do not really believe such nonsense, except at the level of metaphysical cause which points to a transcendent Creator. The taboo does not extend to physical phenomena where cause-effect is the bread and butter of the scientist.

A cause is what produces an effect and an effect is what is produced by a cause. Such a definition makes the two inseparable in the logical order. Logical positivists call that a tautology (that is, a redundancy that tells us nothing); but it is no more tautological than $2+2=4$, and it is much more informative. It supplies the basic rationality for our observation of nature. We understand to the degree that we perceive cause and effect.

It is not always simple. We note, for example, that the acorn is a cause of the oak tree, but it is not the only one even at the physical level. If it were a complete cause, it would already be an oak tree, since the effect is inseparable from its cause. Other partial causes, such as material ingredients and solar energy, are added over time. We note also that the acorn is a "proper" cause only at the level of design, as the depository of the design, not as the intelligent designer. As such it causes the growth to issue in an oak tree rather than a cabbage. The acorn's causation does not reach the transcendent level of goodness or beauty. The tree may exist and still be a poor one. It is also not an adequate cause in the order of existence, since the nature of the acorn does not require that either it or the tree exist. Otherwise all possible acorns, which have the same nature, would already exist, and they would already be oak trees.

Aquinas points out that nothing can cause itself, since it cannot precede itself in the real order. The universal observation is that everything in the world is the effect of something else, and to avoid an infinite series of causes we

124

look to a First Cause different from the ones we observe, a Cause who is not an effect.

This leads us directly to a Catholic doctrine on creation (*Pastoral Constitution on the Church in the Modern World*, No. 36) going back to Saint Augustine, that without the continuous causality of the Creator, the creature would disappear. Since cause and effect are inseparable, if the First Cause is withdrawn, all secondary causes and the universe itself would return to the nothingness from which they came, at once. God not only creates the world but also upholds it and acts as the First Cause of every effect. Thus while he is totally other and transcendent, he maintains immediate contact, a fact obscured by deism and more recently by creationism, which emphasizes single acts of creation and neglects the continuous creative Cause.

• The First Way — The Prime Mover

The first way requires a revamping of Aristotle's ideas of motion, but this is not a great problem. The argument of the first way is that since whatever is moved is moved by another (another rigorous logical connection as it stands), there must be a First Mover somewhere outside the chain of nature who is different, who is unmoved. Otherwise nothing would move. The logic is impeccable, but it does not match the motion we observe in nature. In the Aristotelian scheme, motion continued only as long as the cause was operative, a view which made the flight of an arrow after it left the bow rather awkward to explain. In post-Newtonian physics we think of a change in the state of motion as requiring a "mover" or cause, the "state" of motion not requiring a mover. Energy is conceived as the cause of change in motion, and it is stored as kinetic energy in the inertia of moving objects or as potential energy in the dammed-up forces of gravity and chemical affinity. Saint

Thomas Aquinas would have to translate by calling energy the secondary cause of change of motion, and he would still look to the Primary Cause of all motion and all change. In modern terms, the "Big Bang" did not just happen, and without the sustaining First Cause all energy would disappear with everything else.

Some supplementary arguments often offered for thinking that God exists are: Some things are always true even without a human mind to know them, such as the ratio of the diameter to the circumference of a circle. Like design, this points to an eternal intelligence. Or, we are in pursuit of perfection, and, as Saint Augustine said, "our hearts are restless" until they find perfection in God. This is a more subjective statement of the argument from the transcendent nature of the good. Then people almost universally stand in awe of the holy, the other-worldly. We note, however, that we must be able to distinguish a universal reality from a universal illusion of the human race. Subjective arguments require circumspection.

• Certainty

Saint Thomas Aquinas saw certainty in the five ways, a "necessity in the nature of things to find a first unchanging being, a first efficient cause, a necessary being not from another, one who is supremely being, optimally good, a first intelligent governance, and an ultimate purpose in all things which is God" (*Summa Theologica*, I, q. 2, conclusion of Article 3). Contrast this with his treatment of creation in time (I, q. 46, a. 2), which Aquinas maintained cannot be demonstrated by reason and should not be proposed as a reasoned conclusion lest it give occasion for ridicule. Most of us find it hard to imagine a world of infinite duration, especially in the past. We feel that it ought to have started some time. But reasons are not a matter of imagination or feeling. There is simply nothing about what we know of time or a changing universe that rigorously demands a beginning, as, for example, design requires intelligence or contingent being needs a source in necessary being. So Aquinas concludes that we depend on revelation to know with certainty that the world is not eternal.

The First Vatican Council declared that God can be known by reason with certainty. The Council was preceded by a century or two of erosion of confidence in metaphysical thought of even the household variety like simple cause and effect, and followed by another century that witnessed the eerie scene of serious philosophers dedicating their lives to "overcoming metaphysics" as they understood it. The result is that after the Council defined the possibility of a certain knowledge of God from reason we witness mostly hesitation and doubt on the subject, the fruit of modern "novelties," as Pius XII called them in *Humani Generis* (No. 25).

Certainty comes in various packages. It is primarily in the mind and consists in the evident connection of ideas. By extension it means that the reality represented by these ideas is connected in the same way and will operate accordingly. Absolute certainty we can project in God in whom reality and thought are identical, and our certainty can be considered a participation in divine truth; but the best we have at the human level is logical certainty, more or less immediate and complete and compelling, based on the connection of ideas, ideas which are derived by the fallible process of abstraction from sense perceptions. Once we grasp the idea of two and four and plus and equal, we can have logical certainty that $2+2=4$. The possibility of error lies in misunderstanding the concepts and in lapses of attention, as often happens when adding long columns of figures. Algebra students learn the trick of proving that one equals zero, and then how to find the fallacy. There are ways of cross-checking to arrive at the inner logical certainty.

This human certainty is much broader than mathematics, which is the logic of quantity, and extends to the connection of all ideas. An important example is the logical certainty of the connection between cause and effect, on the understanding that a cause is what produces an effect and an effect is that which is produced by a cause. The uncertainties arise in assigning the concepts to the mixtures of partial and interacting causes we find in the real world.

The certainty of the knowledge of God from reason is a human certainty, with rigorous logic at the core arrived at through a complex learning process. It is difficult enough so that we can appreciate the head start we get from early education and from revelation. While we cannot strictly "believe" on someone else's authority what we already know, we can say in the Creed that we believe in God, since the revealed knowledge is much fuller than natural knowledge and since believing "in God" means more than knowing that he exists. As a preamble to faith our knowledge of God's existence is absorbed into the certainty that comes with the gift of faith which is a share in God's absolute knowledge.

The Council Fathers said we could know with certainty, but they did not say we could prove that God exists, and Aquinas speaks of five "ways" rather than proofs. Proof consists in showing the connection of ideas and demonstrating their validity in the real world. If it also implies trying to convince someone else, then beyond proving theorems in geometry it is seldom successful. Proving that the earth is round to a flat-earthist, evolution to a creationist, creationism to an evolutionist, the existence of God to an atheist, or the carcinogenic effect of tobacco to a smoker, is

128

usually a futile exercise. Beating an adversary over the head with proofs does not bring about a change of heart and is probably counterproductive. But knowing the preambles of faith, especially how God is known from nature, is of great value to Christians, and the pope has made this a topic for general audiences recently.

Two further ideas about proof have emerged in the creationist-evolutionist controversy. One is that evolution lacks scientific verification because the theory cannot predict what will happen next, and prediction is essential for scientific verification. To what extent prediction is essential to scientific verification the reader may judge from a case. A rock collector explores a Mississippian limestone deposit and predicts on the basis of evolutionary theory that he will find fossils of crinoids but not of saber-toothed tigers. At the end of the day his predictions are fulfilled and his companions are impressed. But the theory would have been verified by its simple correspondence with the evidence at the end of the day, even if the rock hunter had not stuck his neck out by making a prediction.

Astronomers predict that they will find something, but they can hardly wait for something new to happen among the stars to verify their science. Evolutionists can sometimes do better. They can predict that radiation will produce new strains of the *Drosophila* fruit fly, but not what they will look like, since by the theory itself the mutations are random. In general, scientific theory is verified by its correspondence with observation. Predictive capacity is a kind of corollary, possible in many instances and rather convincing, but not always necessary. Prediction in evolution is comparable to prediction in historical science (Eldredge, pp. 173ff).

A second idea is borrowed from philosopher of science Sir Karl Popper, who says, ". . . it is the possibility of an empirical refutation that distinguishes empirical or scientific theories" (p. 197). Both creationists and evolutionists point this criterion accusingly at each other. Again refutability is a useful adjunct to the basic verification that comes from matching theory with observation. Discrepancies are easy to spot. If the amateur rock hunter had failed to find a crinoid fossil no one would have been distressed, whereas a single saber-tooth in that location would have caused quite a stir. Creation is supposed to be nonscientific because no one can imagine a way to prove that God did not create species separately. But there are consequences of creationist theory that can be checked, for example, that the earth is only six thousand years old. Creationism is discredited as a science not because it cannot be disproved but because it is so easily disproved: its major theorems do not match the evidence.

• Creation Meets Evolution

The official statements by the Church that science and religion do not conflict do not mean that they should remain aloof. Creation and evolution both give an account of the origin of things, from different starting points and at different levels of understanding. They should complement each other, and occasionally correct each other, as the mechanic and engineer complement and correct each other.

An extreme aloofness on the part of science is expressed in the frequently heard claim that science must practice "systematic" or "postulatory" atheism to pursue knowledge objectively and without preconceptions. Atheism is surely the wrong word here, since atheism means denial of God and is already a preconception, one about which science should not pontificate. If some scientists want atheism, they can have it without hiding behind the skirts of science. The idea of abstracting from a conscious designer in studying evolution has some validity, however, for somewhat the same reason that horses used to be equipped with blinders so they would not be distracted from their course, or startled, or wander off to graze. In this restricted condition they were of course more dependent on a driver with full vision than were horses in the pasture. Human knowledge should be pursued to completion at each appropriate level, and natural science should be free from animism of the kind that supposes divine intervention when the natural process is not understood.

Lack of communication between science and theology is also apparent when in the creationist-evolutionist debate creation is referred to as supernatural. In Catholic usage at least, the word is reserved for the order of grace and redemption. If there is some wondrous phenomenon outside the order of either nature or grace, we call it preternatural. But we say that for creatures to be created is in the order of nature.

Creation and evolution meet beautifully in the expression of biologist Theodosius Dobzhansky: "Evolution is the method whereby Creation is accomplished" (Nogar, 1963, p. 279). A continuous divine causality underlying natural processes which follow the laws created into them gives us a reasonable understanding of creation-evolution. It allows us to see nature evolving upward without getting something for nothing.

If it is hard to follow God's action as he accomplishes his eternal purpose through the laws of chance, we do well to recall a similar mysterious divine action by which he moves our free will. It is Catholic teaching that God not only knows what we are going to choose freely but that he is also the First Cause of our choosing. The philosophical solution is the same: God causes us to act according to our nature, which is to choose freely. In both cases we may

131

argue about the degree of indeterminacy that belongs to the natural process, but ultimately both come to rest on the divine action which recedes into mystery. The Church Fathers said that God's way of creating is incomprehensible, since he is incomprehensible. However, we should not call on mystery where there is only complexity or obscurity. These are rather mysteries of excessive light which continue to respond to further study.

The contribution of evolutionary thought to a Catholic world view is sometimes summarized by saying that Copernicus is a watershed opening up the vast dimensions of space and Darwin is a second watershed opening up the vast dimensions of time. This is a simplification, since Ptolemy had already shifted the roof of the biblical world, the firmament, out as far as the heavenly spheres, and the Judeo-Christian tradition has always been profoundly historical and developmental in its understanding of God's dealings with his people and its hope for the future.

But there is no doubt that the horizon has expanded. As we contemplate the unimaginably vast stellar universe revealed only obscurely by sophisticated instruments and theory and never to be seen by a human eye, and then look for some sense in this extravagant and even playful gesture of creation, we turn to Proverbs 8:30 (and Wisdom, now understood as the divine Son): ". . . I was beside him, like a master workman; and I was daily his delight, rejoicing before him always." Similarly the recently discovered immense age of the universe complements the vastness of space with room for a long, patient preparation for the coming of man and the Son of Man, truly filling out the biblical sense of the "fullness of time" (see Galatians 4:4).

Poetry of course does not prove the theory of evolution, just as Hebrew poetry did not prove the much more restricted cosmogony of the biblical writers. Pagans had great songs for their gods, but the songs did not make their gods real. For cosmogony we need more rigorous thought. But a consideration of the evidence at various levels leads to what seems a sound conclusion, the one known as theistic evolution: that a transcendent Being totally distinct from nature created the universe from nothing and causes it to develop according to the laws he designed into it.

8

Human Origins

Darwin barely mentioned human evolution in *The Origin of Species*, waiting twelve years, until 1871, to take it up in *The Descent of Man*. Wallace left it out entirely. In *Humani Generis* Pope Pius XII first condemned the rampant evolutionary ideologies, then, without mentioning evolution by name, briefly cautioned against swallowing scientific hypotheses that opposed revealed religious doctrine. Finally the pope gave special attention to the "origin of the human body as coming from pre-existing and living matter," suggesting that it be studied with "the greatest moderation and caution." Evolution of the stars and of plant and animal life can be viewed with a certain detachment. The proposal that the human race has descended, or even ascended, from brute species has always stirred up much opposition. Politeness to the human race suggests that the main points of the case be given a separate chapter.

At the level of natural science we are confronted with fossils. The first to attract widespread attention to human origins was found in 1857 in a cave in the Neander Valley of the Düssel River just above its confluence with the Rhine. The find consisted of some bones of a beetle-browed individual whose exaggerated reconstruction gives us the popular image of brutish Neanderthal man. More remains of the same type have been found in other parts of Europe as well as in Asia and Africa, and it turns out that Neanderthal had a somewhat larger brain case than the rest of us.

Eugène Dubois, armed with the hypothesis that the closest relatives of mankind were the orangutan and the gibbon, searched their habitats in the East Indies and in the 1890s uncovered in Java some bones which he assigned to an apelike creature he called *Pithecanthropus* ("ape-man"), more commonly known as Java man. Later specimens from the same region were more nearly human and were assigned to the *Homo erectus* stock.

There were a few more scattered finds before Piltdown man turned up in Sussex around 1912. The Piltdown "fossil" — as mentioned earlier, in Chapter 6 — consisted of part of a human skull, relatively recent, along with part of the jawbone of a chimpanzee with teeth carefully filed to fit the skull, and all stained to match the older animal fossils in the same deposit. The hoax was not discovered definitively until 1954, but there were plenty of skeptics. I distinctly recall a lively argument on evolution in 1940 during which I was informed that the Piltdown man was a fake. The source quoted was the curator of the Cleveland Museum of Natural History in private conversation. Nevertheless the "fossil" was accepted by the highest authority or at least kept on hold for forty-one years and remains a warning to observe sober caution when dealing with fossils.

During the 1920s and 1930s, extensive excavations in northern China — in which Father Pierre Teilhard de Chardin took a major part — uncovered the remains of Peking man. The treasure itself was lost in transit in 1941, but casts and detailed records allow him to be studied and classified as *Homo erectus*, along with Java man.

In the meantime Raymond Dart had discovered the Taung baby in the dolomite quarry of a limeworks in South Africa, and the African saga of our apelike ancestors began to unfold. The work in South Africa was continued by Robert Broom and gave us *Australopithecus* ("southern ape"), a creature that walked upright, had humanlike teeth, and had about half the minimum cranial capacity of modern humans. There are two australopithecine lines, the light form called *gracilis* and the heavier *robustus*.

Louis Leakey began his archaeological explorations of East Africa in 1926 and soon found quantities of simple chipped stone tools in Olduvai Gorge, part of the great Rift Valley which was to be a rich source of intriguing fossils. On July 17, 1959, his wife, Mary, found a complete skull of the *Australopithecus* type associated with the primitive tools in deposits dated by the potassium-argon method at 1.75 million years. Louis Leakey took the skull with him to the Darwin centennial celebration at the University of Chicago in November of that year. A stone circle suggesting a home base pointed to further human activity at this remote period. In 1960 the Leakeys discovered the remains of the somewhat larger-brained *Homo habilis*, then some of *Homo erectus*, who was about 1.2 million years old. Further discoveries rewarded the efforts of Richard Leakey, who continued and further publicized the work of his parents.

In 1974 Chicago-born Dr. Donald Johanson created

another sensation by coming up with Lucy in Ethiopia, forty percent of the skeleton of an adult female about three and a half feet tall, and the next year the bones of a group of somewhat larger individuals, the "Family," with generally human features but without tools nearby, all about three million years old.

A somewhat nebulous *Ramapithecus*, bearing the name of the Hindu hero-god Rama and unearthed in Pakistan and other places, allows the tentative (Remember Piltdown!) proposal of a family tree for the human species. Hominids branched off from the simian line in *Ramapithecus*, which gave rise to three branches, the two australopithecine lines, *robustus* and *gracilis* (later becoming extinct along with the parent branch), and a third branch, *Homo habilis* (later developing into *Homo erectus* and then *Homo sapiens*). This in turn branched into the three principal races we know before Neanderthals went their separate way and became extinct. The Cro-Magnon artists who painted in caves some tens of thousands of years ago belong to the *Homo sapiens* group, often called *Homo sapiens sapiens*.

Few predictions can be more confidently made than that this hypothetical family tree will undergo further evolution, perhaps changing beyond recognition. But the fossils will still be there, probably supplemented by many more, and they will never fit into a six-thousand-year creationist scheme. They fit the hypothesis, based on evolutionary theory, that the human species evolved from older and now extinct primate species.

This hypothesis is supported by the morphology of contemporary living things. The human body shares with all earth life the peculiar cell structure which is regenerated on the DNA template. It shares sense organs with the animal kingdom, a skeleton with the vertebrates, and bodily

137

Ramapithecus
13 million years

Australopithecus africanus [gracilis]
3 m.

Australopithecus boisei [robustus]
3 m.

6 m.

......

Homo habilis ——— Homo erectus ——— Homo sapiens
3 m.   .5 m.

100,000 yrs.

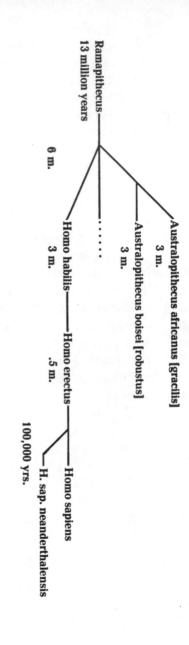

Ramapithecus ——— Australopithecus afarensis ——— Aust. africanus ——— Aust. robustus
8 m.   4 m.   2.5 m.   1.5 m.

H. sap. neanderthalensis

H. habilis
2 m.

H. erectus
1 m.

H. sapiens
.5 m.

Two human-family trees (based on graphs appearing in Origins, by Richard Leakey and Roger Lewin [top graph], and Lucy, by Donald Johanson [bottom graph]) organs and members (some of them vestigial) with mammals. Its upright stance, manual dexterity, and brain development are foreshadowed but not matched by the apes. We hear that "there is less genetic difference between man and chimpanzee than between fox and dog" (Ruse, p. 237). Creationists say the Creator was merely using economy of means in making all animals alike, but a common origin is a much better hypothesis if biblical literalism does not stand in the way.

There are enough problems, however, even at the level of archaeology. The fossils are numerous and impressive, until we consider the long time span, the geographical area, and the extensive bodily changes they are supposed to cover. William R. Fix underscores some of the difficulties. The African finds have two divergent interpretations, British (Richard Leakey) and American (Donald Johanson) (see the preceding illustration). *Australopithecus* has been reconstructed with faces ranging from pure ape to pure human. Fix remarks, "The fossil record pertaining to man is still so sparsely known that those who insist on positive declarations can do nothing more than jump from one hazardous surmise to another and hope that the next dramatic discovery does not make them utter fools" (p. 150).

As we raise our sights from the biological to the anthropological level, we look for historical evidence of a human kind of intelligence, for the idealization of experience, not just toolmaking for use but making beautiful tools, not just clever and cooperative hunting as found in a pride of lions but the hunt idealized in song and dance. We find this kind of record in cave paintings, most strikingly in Europe. Neanderthals in Asia Minor reveal a human self-consciousness as they prepare graves for a life after death, while early samples of statuary hint at a capacity for transcendent

139

thought reaching out to a reality beyond physical nature. We wonder whether such a transition was gradual or abrupt, or whether there is a level at which gradualism is excluded (Deely, p. 137). Evolution must be said to give an incomplete answer at the human level (Nogar, p. 208).

If we look at the present we find three major racial divisions of the species, with several dozen subgroups, all quite human. All intermarry freely if social bias is set aside. The infants of one culture adapt easily to another, so there is no difference in basic capacity even though physical differences remain. What is striking is that no other animal group stands anywhere close to humanity in this kind of capacity, as experiments with apes show clearly enough. Chimpanzees are as keen at their own game as we are, but the world of abstract ideas does not open to them. They do not learn to speak by simple observation as children do, nor do they establish schools to study man and other animals.

For comparison we may consider that chimpanzees, gibbons, gorillas, and orangutans are members of distinct biological species, but all stand at the same general level of animal intelligence. If the human race evolved in a parallel fashion, where are the sibling species, species of comparable human intelligence? The hypothesis that seems most probable is that at some time in the past, long enough to allow the evolution of the separate races, there was a clean break of *Homo sapiens* from all other lines. How this may have happened the evidence does not suggest, so the imagination has free rein once again.

The arguments about what should be called separate species, whether by biologists or philosophers, are of perennial interest. We may say that species are not arbitrary mental categories but are the result of a valid abstraction from the real world with arbitrarily chosen limits. The

140

shepherd dog is really different from the wolf, and biologists choose as an intelligible dividing line natural mating habits. Of course dogs may not be paying attention all the time, and we are reminded that abstraction is not a perfect handle on reality.

More important is determining what is human. At different levels the human species can be recognized by an opposable thumb and upright stance, toolmaking ability, a lower limit of brain size, language, abstract thought, self-consciousness with awareness of immortality, artistic sensitivity and idealization, moral sense, and awareness of a transcendent God. An unborn or newborn child does not use its higher intelligence, and most of us use it rather sparingly; but the inner reality, consisting of human nature and the human soul, is already there with the potential for fully human activity. There is no gradualism at this level in the case of the individual. How it happened in history is the unanswered question.

• Scripture

Catholic scholars interpret the Genesis story of our first parents much as they do the rest of the creation account. They first point to the literary characteristics of the story as a key to its understanding, especially the evidence of two sources. Chapter 1 has God speak of creating man in his image, while Chapter 2 has him form man (*adham*) from dust (*adhama*) as a potter might, then breathe the breath of life into him. Chapter 1 has the whole earth prepared ahead of time and consigned to the man with no mention of Eden, while Chapter 2 has Eden planted after Adam was already on hand. The first chapter says God created them male and female, while the second makes a dramatic afterthought of Eve and has her formed from Adam's rib, after which Adam sings the "rib song" for good measure: "This at last is bone of my bones, and flesh of my flesh; she shall be called Woman, because she was taken out of Man" (Genesis 2:23). The message of this episode may simply be that man and woman have one nature and are therefore suitable mates. The overall message is that God created our first parents and that they were aware of his special care and his authority. They spoke to him and he spoke to them. The report is couched in the popular language of remembered stories. To insist on the details of the stories is to read a message the author did not intend.

Christian scholars have made progress in blending revelation and science in the knowledge of origins, a process that calls for "the greatest moderation and caution," in the words of *Humani Generis*, and the greatest patience, we may add some thirty-five years later. For a theological overview the reader may consult the little book by Zachary Hayes, O.F.M., *What Are They Saying About Creation?* Here we shall consider two special concerns of Pope Pius XII: (1) that Genesis is "history in the true sense" and (2) the question of monogenesis versus polygenesis, which has a bearing on the Fall and Redemption.

• History in the True Sense

What is meant by "history in the true sense" may first be tested on the neutral ground of the story of Caesar's crossing the Rubicon. While it is the decisive step toward the Roman Empire, it is unlikely to stir up religious controversy in our time.

First, an eyewitness account could report details like whether the army swam, crossed in boats, or waded, whether by day or by night, in army array or in small groups. The eyewitness might observe many such things but see nothing more significant than another army trampling his fields.

142

Second, a senator from Rome, not an eyewitness, would investigate and report the incident as a defiance of the Republic and would note details that revealed Caesar's attitude and capabilities.

Third, a historian of the modern persuasion would be busy with the recorded facts and with archaeological evidence from the site, if he could find it, and would interpret the event in terms of the later development of the Roman imperial tradition.

Fourth, a novelist could fill in the details of things that had to happen in one way or another, such as the options for crossing the river, and he could supply dialogue. Two novelists could contradict each other, one saying it was by day and the other by night, without distorting the basic historical fact that Caesar crossed the Rubicon.

Fifth, a widow whose husband did not return might depict him as crossing in shining armor. Her children would understand her even if later they discovered he was not wearing armor.

Finally, a theorist with his own axe to grind might make a study of ancient myths and conclude that Caesar never crossed the Rubicon at all, and that the whole affair was "historical" only in the sense that later emperors explained their place in history by means of the legend. This interpretation of literary genres would hold that the story is a "true" myth expressing the faith of the Roman people.

History as recorded in the Bible obviously has a wide range of styles, and the pope leaves it to scholars to find the proper interpretation in particular cases. Some of the travels of Saint Paul are recorded as eyewitness accounts in Acts. The stories of David, some of the greatest narratives in all literature, seem to have been written down in Solomon's time, and they show some of the freedom of the historical novel. It would be an abuse of historical evidence

143

to state categorically that Job never existed, but his existence in history has no bearing on the book that bears his name. We have no problem seeing Christ's parables as fiction teaching a lesson.

The importance of understanding how the Bible records history lies in the fact that Christianity is a historical religion, not a mythological one. It is founded on God's revelation of his actual dealings with his people. To deny what is divinely revealed as history is to deny the faith. In the extreme case, to reduce the story of the Resurrection of Christ to an expression of the faith of the early Christian communities, thus treating New Testament history as the theorist above treated the story of Caesar, is to destroy Christianity utterly. We may as well go back to the song and dance of our pagan ancestors — and that has also been proposed seriously.

The history of creation is unique, so the Genesis narrative does not fit easily into familiar categories. The sacred author knew that creation happened, but there were no eyewitnesses, so he related the history, not in myths which do not suppose real events, but in narratives that clothe real events, in stories that the people were used to hearing, as people were once used to hearing about soldiers in shining armor. In *Humani Generis* the Holy Father leaves it to exegetes to determine how history is narrated in the various parts of the Bible, and we can expect further refinements.

• Monogenism — Polygenism

God has revealed, as handed down in Scripture and Tradition and taught by the Church, that he made man and woman and gave them a command which they disobeyed. The question raised by the modern theory of evolution is whether there were just two people involved. *Humani*

Generis puts it this way: "When, however, there is question of another conjectural opinion, namely, polygenism, the children of the Church by no means enjoy such liberty. For the faithful cannot embrace that opinion which maintains that after Adam there existed on this earth true men who did not take their origin through natural generation from him as from the first parent of all, or that Adam represents a certain number of first parents. Nor is it in any way apparent how such an opinion can be reconciled with that which the sources of revealed truth and the documents of the teaching authority of the Church propose with regard to original sin, which proceeds from sin actually committed by an individual Adam and which through generation is passed on to all and is in everyone as his own" (No. 66).

Since 1950, theologians have tried to make it apparent how polygenism could be reconciled with revelation, but in 1966 Pope Paul VI indicated that the doctrine of original sin was still a matter of concern. While theologians speculate on their lofty plane, we may descend to a more mundane level and imagine the various ways in which the human race might have appeared on the earth, with no concrete evidence to impede our fancy.

1. At one extreme would be straight evolution. *Homo erectus* gradually evolved a bigger and better brain and became *Homo sapiens*, with no Adam, no Eve, and no original sin. The main advantage of this simple view is that it does not require the theory of evolution to bend. The theory has had to bend so often lately that this no longer seems a great advantage. This scenario neglects important empirical data, in particular the sharp genetic and intellectual isolation of the human species already referred to. There are no human-brute hybrids except in mythology. It also passes over the perversity of custom and moral degeneracy found only in the human species and all over the world as

though coming from a common source. In other words, original sin even in its evident effects does not fit into this simple hypothesis.

2. A minor modification touching on the races defines polygenism as "the scientific theory that the various human races derived from parallel lines that separated from the common stock before attaining humanhood, a theory for which at present there is no shadow of scientific proof" (G. Vandenbroek, in Ryan, p. 18).

3. As another possibility let us suppose that among the "creatures" living at a certain time just two, Adam and Eve, were selected to know God and speak to him with a familiarity that the Bible associated with the beginning of our species. Father Nogar (1963, p. 381) even asks whether it was an embryo or a full-grown primate that received the first human soul. Once this happened, the present population of the world would all be descended from them by the sure mathematics of pair bonding, in which the number of ancestors is 2^n (n being the number of generations). In forty generations (about a thousand years), this gives 2^{40}, or 10^{12}, one trillion ancestors. There would be duplication, but still no one could miss being descended from the Adam and Eve of this version. A drawback of this idea is that we would all be descendants of Adam's neighbors as well, with a genetic input from them in proportion to their numbers.

4. Another hypothesis would have Adam and Eve represent a number of people, a choice explicitly criticized in the quotation from *Humani Generis* as clouding over the doctrine of original sin. A group isolated for a sufficient time could with some strain be imagined as receiving human endowments while other hominoids died out. But if original sin is to be inherited, or even passed on by moral influence, the group would have to be small. Why not reduce it to a single pair?

146

5. The next version would have this single pair born of prehuman primates and then called, somewhat as Abraham was called, to be ancestors of the human race, receiving all human endowments. Their ancestors and siblings would conveniently die off and avoid cohabitation with the humans. Perhaps they were wiped out by some catastrophe which spared the chosen pair, who then found their way to Eden.

6. That brings us to the other extreme: Adam formed miraculously. There are two possibilities: either that Adam and Eve were simply created in God's image (Genesis 1:27), or that Adam was formed from dust and Eve from Adam's rib (Genesis 2:7, 21ff). A creationist proposal (Parker, p. 80) is that they had all the racial genes so that the races could descend from them without mutation. This hypothesis has the advantage of simple correspondence with the Genesis story, although it requires choosing between the first- and second-chapter versions. It has the fault of being not a true literal reading of the Bible but a misreading, as Rahner says. The creation chapters present a serious historical event in terms of folk traditions in popular language the people were used to hearing, including the starry firmament, the six-day workweek, a talking serpent whose natural-looking crawl was the result of a curse as in animal fables, a commandment in the image of forbidden fruit, and a tree of life. Among other folklore elements we find God walking, breathing, planting trees, and molding clay (Maher, p. 34). The sacred author molded these things with consummate art and sophistication and surely did not expect the details of the stories to be interpreted with naïve literalness. This version also neglects the fossils, or supposes that they were created to simulate the bones of human ancestors.

It should be clear from this exercise in fantasy that

there is much we do not know about these far-off days. Revelation assures us that Creation and the Fall are historical events, not myths. Archaeology has turned up many bones, but the chances that Adam's bones will be found are remote indeed. With the information provided by the two sources, science and revelation, scholars will continue to speculate and there will probably be more breakthroughs, but like Saint John Chrysostom we do not expect to learn everything.

• More Questions — Suffering

Information pointing to human evolution raises a number of philosophical and theological questions. The immortality of the intellectual soul, defined as a dogma of Catholic faith by the Fifth Lateran Council of 1512-1517 (Denzinger, 738), is also known from reason. The mind lives naturally with ideas, and ideas embrace changing things in a timeless way. The human mind, and therefore that side of human nature which has this mental capacity, stands free of change and of time which is the measure of change. The question arises: When does this immortal soul appear in history? We hold that it is created in the individual at the moment of conception, even though the intellectual powers develop only gradually throughout life. This leaves us somewhat uneasy about the immortal souls of the unborn dead, and we tell ourselves to leave such things in the hands of God. Now evolution extends the same dilemma to the souls of the early toolmakers.

Essential to revelation about our first parents is the call to grace from which they fell, their supernatural friendship with God. Redemption from their fall is the very heart of Christianity. The tradition includes vaguely defined preternatural gifts such as freedom from death and from suffering, which do not fit smoothly into an evolutionary

148

scheme. (Several Councils took up the question of pre-ternatural gifts and left it unfinished.) Some theologians solve the problem by saying that the preternatural gifts were inoperative, never more than a promise, since they disappeared with the Fall (Metz, pp. 144ff), but that is hardly the final solution.

Some creationists say that all suffering and death, even of animals, began with the Fall, citing Romans 5:12, "sin came into the world through one man and death through sin," and they use this as an argument for a six-day creation (Morris, 1972, p. 77). They condemn the evolution which would make the Creator a "sadistic God" (Morris, 1966, p. 34) who causes animals to suffer pain over billions of years without some reason like human sin. Evolutionists like Darwin (Gould, Ch. 2; Futuyma, p. 198) go in the other direction, abandoning God and keeping evolution. When they consider the apparently senseless suffering in the world, they conclude that God is not very good, or is not capable of preventing suffering, or is nonexistent. They were not the first by any means to go that way. Lucretius did it, as we saw, in *De Rerum Natura.*

There are various ways of applying salve to the painful thought. Nature lovers point out that when a deer has its bowels torn out by wolves, it goes into a state of shock and really does not suffer much. On the other hand, running from pain is how animals escape injury, so pain is really good for them. Of course this supposes that they live wide-eyed with fear of pain. If compassionate human beings had planned the world, they would have tried to achieve the good result by less distressing means. Earthbound thought faces a real dilemma in animal and human suffering, and its best advice is to keep a stiff upper lip.

From a more philosophical perspective we have seen that created things are imperfect by necessity, since their nature cannot have the perfection of existence from itself and needs to be created. Saint Augustine said that evil springs from the fact that creatures come out of nothingness (O'Toole, p. 9). But why this kind of imperfection? Why pain? We proceed to paraphrase the scriptural saying: "Does the pot say to the potter, why have you made me thus?" (See Isaiah 29:16.) Evolutionary theory reinforces the philosophical and theological consideration that God wills nature to develop according to its own laws, which involve an element of chance. This development has included suffering. He wills the good and permits the evil that comes with it. All this is intellectually acceptable but does not soothe the compassionate heart.

Christian faith finds its answer in the Incarnation and Redemption, but it is not an easy one. The God revealed in the Incarnation is a dynamic God, whose nature is love, the total self-giving of Father and Son in the Spirit of communion. Total love means total detachment, as Christian mysticism has realized, and when the Son became man he embraced the suffering and death that made that detachment real in his human life. The "baptism" of blood and the cross were the realization of our Lord's total love. Animal and human suffering arising out of the necessary imperfection of nature as well as human sin thus enters into the long anticipation of the Incarnation and its realization of love. The Christian teaching is that God brings good out of evil in the Redemption. This is strong drink, and the Christian struggles to accept it in his own life. Buddha thought of overcoming suffering by overcoming desire. The Christian embraces it with desire, in faith if not always enthusiastically. So while superficially impugning the divine attribute of goodness, suffering corrects our insight into divine goodness and reveals the divine flame.

Evolution and suffering meet in other ways. At times

150

we hear the proud boast that with the advent of genetic engineering mankind is taking charge of its own evolution, presumably to produce a master race or at least one free from disease. Coming in alongside this boast is an expression of regret that curing diseases one by one in people leads to a deterioration of the human gene pool by allowing disease-prone specimens to reproduce themselves. There is no cause to quarrel with the effort to diminish suffering even wholesale by eliminating entire species of obnoxious parasites or by building up a resistance to disease by a certain genetic control which stays within the limits of moral behavior and respects human dignity. The human race has always shown a legitimate interest in "good breeding."

Yet a realistic assessment of history suggests avoiding inflated expectations about what mankind will achieve in doing away with suffering. Furthermore Christian faith dashes some cold water on evolutionistic futurism by looking for a "new heaven and a new earth," at the end of the world as we know it.

Natural evolution has not changed the human species noticeably, in the opinion of at least some evolutionists, since the time of Cro-Magnon man. In any case social evolution has outstripped it. Social evolution in its best sense has brought us to live together through mutual help, the strong supporting the weak, those who are healthy tending the sick. The Christian vision is not only to work for a better world within realistic limits but also to look beyond to a higher ideal in which those who feed the hungry or spend their lives caring for the handicapped invert the situation and bring good from evil, so becoming perfect as their heavenly Father is perfect.

Evolution has been called the greatest discovery of the human mind, but that is an exaggeration. The historical dimension it adds is very important, but its greatest significance lies in complementing the still greater discovery of the life of the spirit, which enables us to understand and embrace history and all of reality at a level that transcends time and history. The beginning of this spiritual awareness is lost in the deep past and it was developed in all civilizations. Both discoveries are great to the extent that they implement the greatest discovery of all: that man can know God and answer his call as we learn from the Book of Genesis; that man can understand where he came from and where he is going; and that man can know God's dealings in nature and history and enter into them. To the extent that evolutionary ideology has tried to undermine this highest human enterprise it has been a long step backward.

Afterword

The creationist-evolutionist controversy became a political and social issue in this country with the enactment of state laws forbidding the teaching of evolution in public schools, followed by laws requiring that scientific creationism be taught there. Constitutional considerations and good sense have eliminated both kinds of laws. But the struggle goes on, and fundamentalism gains ground even among Catholics. These pages were written with high respect for the sincerity and sturdy faith of creationists, but with the intention of showing that their theology is misguided and their creation science a disaster. The harm to religion arises not from the fact that people believe in a six-day creation, a six-thousand-year-old world, a flat earth, a solid firmament, or geocentrism, but that these things are taught as being required by divine revelation, thus bringing down ridicule on revelation as Saint Augustine saw long ago. The effects of creationism are of course benign compared to the destructive ideology of materialistic evolutionism.

Catholics have a better way. They listen to the voice of the living Church which has sorted out the situation and accepts from afar a moderate theory of evolution, along with such theories as relativity and indeterminacy, respecting the autonomy of science in its own domain but not giving human theory more than its due. The details of the origin of the human race remain obscure, as they were for the Fathers of the Church, and we are not in a hurry to force the issue.

Fundamentalists claim they learn the answers by reading the Bible, but we are all people of the Good Book. Even before the age of printing and general literacy the faithful were educated in and through the Bible, as is evident from the liturgy, Christian art, and the sermons of the Fathers.

The twentieth century offers not only printing but an explosive expansion of intellectual activity in all directions. We have all been immersed in it or at least exposed to it through a much longer formal education than our ancestors and need a counterbalance of spiritual thought and wisdom to keep our feet and avoid being swept away, to keep pace in the knowledge of what it is all for, where we came from and where we are going. The Bible can continue to be the inspired source of this kind of wisdom, provided it is read. And no one learns to read anything, especially the Bible, without help from the experience of others. Biblical scholarship has kept pace with the knowledge explosion, and, among the useful commentaries available, a book like Bruce Vawter's *A Path Through Genesis* is a great help in the area we are concerned with. It all suggests a lifelong adult education project aimed at lifelong spiritual growth. As a bonus it should provide a response when Johnny or Jenny comes home from evolution class parroting a teacher who says the Bible is wrong.

The central lesson for the modern reader coming out of biblical scholarship seems to be: the windows to the divine message are the human authors, who were skilled writers in a highly sophisticated tradition. We try to put ourselves in their sandals, try to find out where they are coming from and what they mean to say. There is both a negative and a positive aspect to this.

The negative lesson, important in the understanding of the creation narrative, is that God did not correct everything in the background of the human writer or his culture. He did not supply a perfect language but used Hebrew, Aramaic, and Greek. He did not reveal a new cosmology, whether that of the Greeks, or Copernicus, or quasars, or of the year A.D. 4000, which we cannot even imagine yet, but spoke as the Hebrews spoke about the world. He did not even correct the limited moral judgment which seems to accept polygamy and even more scandalous behavior. The divine message is transmitted without error through common speech, just as a scientist speaks without error of the sunset even though he knows that the sun does not do the moving.

Positively this attention to the human author invites us into the whole Bible from "In the beginning" of Genesis to the "Amen" of Revelation. Not just the momentarily inspiring passages or useful quotations but the whole history of God's dealing with his people, the successes and sordid failures, the superficially irrelevant genealogies and familiar tales — all of these belong to this total message to us, a message so rich in divine wisdom and human response and experience. In our growth through the Bible we are led not by fundamentalist interpretation or even by good scholarship but by the Spirit in the living and teaching Church.

Bibliography

Allen, Don Cameron. *The Legend of Noah*. Champaign, Ill.: University of Illinois Press, 1963.

Aquinas, St. Thomas. *Summa Theologica*.

Augustine, St. *The Literal Meaning of Genesis*. Tr. John Hammond Taylor, S.F. Westminster, Md.: The Newman Press, 1982.

Bohm, David. *Causality and Chance in Modern Physics*. Philadelphia, Pa.: University of Pennsylvania Press, 1971.

Boller, Paul F. *American Thought in Transition*. Lanham, Md.: University Press of America, 1981.

Born, Max. *The Natural Philosophy of Cause and Chance*. New York, N.Y.: Dover Publications, 1964.

Burtt, Edwin Arthur. *The Metaphysical Foundations of Modern Science*. Garden City, N.Y.: Doubleday, 1954.

Clark, Ronald. *The Survival of Charles Darwin*. New York, N.Y.: Random House, 1984.

Crombie, A.C. *Augustine to Galileo*. Cambridge, Mass.: Harvard University Press, 1953.

Dampier, William C. *A History of Science*. New York: N.Y.: Cambridge University Press, 1961.

Darwin, Charles. *The Origin of Species*. New York, N.Y.: New American Library, 1957.

_____. *The Descent of Man*. New York, N.Y.: D. Appleton, 1873.

_____. *Autobiography*. New York, N.Y.: W.W. Norton, 1969.

Daschbach, Edward, S.V.D. "Catholics and Creationism," *Our Sunday Visitor*, October 21, 1984.

Deely, John, and Nogar, Raymond. *The Problem of Evolution*. East Norwalk, Conn.: Appleton-Century-Crofts, 1973.

Denzinger, Henricus. *Enchiridion Symbolorum*. Freiburg, Germany: Herder, 1946.

Ditfurth, Hoimar von. *The Origins of Life*. San Francisco, Calif.: Harper and Row, 1982.

Dobzhansky, Theodosius. *Mankind Evolving*. New Haven, Conn.: Yale University Press, 1962.

Duggan, G.H., S.M. *Teilhardism and the Faith*. Cork, Ireland: The Mercier Press, 1968.

Ehrensvärd, Gösta. *Life, Origin and Development*. Chicago, Ill.: University of Chicago Press, Phoenix Books, 1960.

Eiseley, Loren. *Darwin's Century*. Garden City, N.Y.: Doubleday, Anchor Books, 1958.

Eldredge, Niles. *Time Frames*. New York, N.Y.: Simon and Schuster, 1985.

Filby, Frederick. *The Flood Reconsidered*. London, England: Pickering, 1970.

Fix, William R. *The Bone Peddlers*. New York, N.Y.: Macmillan, 1984.

Fothergill, P.G. *Evolution and Christians*. Newcastle-on-Tyne, England: Longman's, 1961.

Fraine, Jean de, S.J. *The Bible and the Origin of Man*. New York, N.Y.: Desclee, 1962.

Friar, Wayne, and Davis, Percival. *A Case for Creation*. Chicago, Ill.: Moody Press, 1983.

Frye, Roland, ed. *Is God a Creationist?* New York, N.Y.: Charles Scribner's Sons, 1983.

Futuyma, Douglas. *Science on Trial*. New York, N.Y.: Pantheon Books, 1983.

Gilkey, Langdon. *Maker of Heaven and Earth*. Garden City, N.Y.: Doubleday, 1959.

Gillespie, Charles C. *Genesis and Geology*. Cambridge, Mass.: Harvard University Press, 1951.

Gish, Duane T. *Evolution? The Fossils Say No!* San Diego, Calif.: Creation Life Publishers, 1978.

_____. "It is Either 'In the Beginning, God,' . . . or . . . 'Hydrogen,' " *Christianity Today*, October 8, 1982.

Godfrey, Laurie, ed. *Scientists Confront Creationism*. New York, N.Y.: W.W. Norton, 1983.

Gould, Stephen Jay. *Hen's Teeth and Horse's Toes*. New York: N.Y. W.W. Norton, 1983.

Gruber, Jacob W. *A Conscience in Conflict*. New York, N.Y.: Columbia University Press, 1960.

Haigh, Paula. *Thirty Theses Against Theistic Evolution*. Louisville, Ky.: The Catholic Center for Creation Research, 1976.

Hall, Marshall and Sandra. *The Truth: God or Evolution*. Grand Rapids, Mich.: Baker Book House, 1975.

Hauret, Charles. *Beginnings: Genesis and Modern Science*. Dubuque, Ia.: Priory Press, 1955.

Hayes, Zachary, O.F.M. *What Are They Saying About Creation?* Ramsey, N.J.: Paulist Press, 1980.

Hessler, Bertram. *The Bible in the Light of Modern Science*. Chicago, Ill.: Franciscan Herald Press, 1960.

Hick, John, ed. *The Existence of God*. New York, N.Y.: Macmillan, 1964.

Hoyle, Fred. *The Intelligent Universe*. New York, N.Y.: Holt, Rinehart and Winston, 1983.

Hull, David L. *Darwin and His Critics*. Cambridge, Mass.: Harvard University Press, 1973.

Hulsbosch, A., O.S.A. *God in Creation and Evolution*. New York, N.Y.: Sheed and Ward, 1965.

Hume, David. *Enquiries Concerning the Human Understanding and Concerning the Principles of Morals*. Oxford, England: Oxford University Press, 1902.

Indicopleustes, Cosmas. *Christian Topography*. New York, N.Y.: Burt Franklin, 1897.

Jaki, Stanley L. *Angels, Apes, and Men*. LaSalle, Ill.: Sherwood Sugden, 1983.

Johanson, Donald C. *Lucy*. New York, N.Y.: Simon and Schuster, 1981.

Johnson, J.W.G. *The Crumbling Theory of Evolution*. Brisbane, Australia, 1981.

Kaiser, Edwin, C.PP.S. "Before Teilhard there was Herman Schell," *American Ecclesiastical Review*, May 1972.

King, Thomas, S.J. *Teilhard and the Unity of Knowledge*. Ramsey, N.J.: Paulist Press, 1983.

Kitcher, P. *Abusing Science, the Case Against Creationism*. Cambridge, Mass.: MIT Press, 1982.

Lammerts, Walter, comp. *Why Not Creation?* Nutley, N.J.: Presbyterian Reformed Publishing Company, 1970.

_____. *Scientific Studies in Special Creation*. Nutley, N.J.: Presbyterian Reformed Publishing Company, 1971.

Leakey, Richard. *Origins*. New York, N.Y.: E. P. Dutton, 1977.

_____. *People of the Lake*. Garden City, N.Y.: Doubleday, 1978.

Litynski, Zygmunt. "Should We Burn Darwin?" *Science Digest*, January 1961.

Lucas, Mary and Ellen. *Teilhard*. Garden City, N.Y.: Doubleday, 1977.

Lucretius. *De Rerum Natura*.

Lunn, Arnold. *The Revolt Against Reason*. London, England: Eyre & Spottiswoode, 1950.

Luyten, Norbert, O.P. "Teilhard de Chardin: Eine Neue Synthese des Wissens?" *Heilpaedagogische Werkblaetter*, March 1963.

Maher, Michael, M.S.C. *The Old Testament Message, Genesis.* Wilmington, Del.: Michael Glazer, 1882.

Mayr, Ernst. *Animal Species and Evolution.* Cambridge, Mass.: Harvard University Press, 1963.

Messenger, Ernest. *Evolution and Theology.* New York, N.Y.: Macmillan, 1932.

————, ed. *Theology and Evolution.* Westminster, Md.: The Newman Press, 1949.

Metz, Johannes, ed. *The Evolving World and Theology.* Ramsey, N.J.: Paulist Press, 1967.

Mivart, St. George Jackson. *Lessons from Nature.* New York, N.Y.: D. Appleton, 1876.

Molloy, Gerald. *Geology and Revelation.* New York, N.Y.: G.P. Putnam's Sons, 1870.

Monod, Jacques. *Chance and Necessity.* New York, N.Y.: Alfred Knopf, 1971.

Montagu, Ashley, ed. *Science and Creationism.* New York, N.Y.: Oxford University Press, 1984.

Moore, James. *The Post Darwinian Controversies.* New York, N.Y.: Cambridge University Press, 1979.

Morris, Henry. *The Twilight of Evolution.* Grand Rapids, Mich.: Baker Book House, 1963.

————. *Studies in the Bible and Science.* Phillipsburg, N.J.: Presbyterian Reformed Publishing Company, 1966.

————. *Evolution and the Modern Christian.* Phillipsburg, N.J.: Presbyterian Reformed Publishing Company, 1967.

————, and Whitcomb, John. *The Genesis Flood.* Phillipsburg, N.J.: Presbyterian Reformed Publishing Company, 1969.

————. *The Remarkable Birth of Planet Earth.* Minneapolis, Minn.: Dimension Books, 1972.

————. *Scientific Creationism.* San Diego, Calif.: Creation Life Publishers, 1974.

————. *The Troubled Waters of Evolution.* San Diego, Calif.: Creation Life Publishers, 1975.

————. *The Beginning of the World.* Denver, Colo.: Accent Books, 1977.

————. *That You Might Believe.* San Diego, Calif.: Creation Life Publishers, 1978.

_____. *The Scientific Case for Creation*. San Diego, Calif.: Creation Life Publishers, 1981.

_____, and Parker, Gary. *What Is Creation Science?* San Diego, Calif.: Master Book Publishers, 1982.

_____. *A History of Modern Creationism*. San Diego, Calif.: Master Book Publishers, 1984.

Mynarek, Hubertus. *Der Mensch, Sinnziel der Weltentwicklung*. Munich, Germany: Verlag Ferdinand Schoningh, 1967.

Newman, John Henry. *Letters and Diaries*. Oxford, England: Oxford University Press, 1973.

Nogar, Raymond, O.P. *The Wisdom of Evolution*. Garden City, N.Y.: Doubleday, 1963.

_____. *The Lord of the Absurd*. New York, N.Y.: Herder and Herder, 1966.

Ong, Walter, S.J., ed. *Darwin's Vision and Christian Perspective*. New York, N.Y.: Macmillan, 1960.

O'Toole, Christopher, C.S.C. *The Philosophy of Creation in the Writings of St. Augustine*. Washington, D.C.: Catholic University of America Press, 1944.

Parker, Gary. *Creation, the Facts of Life*. San Diego, Calif.: Creation Life Publishers, 1980.

Patten, Donald. *The Biblical Flood and the Ice Epoch*. Seattle, Wash.: Pacific Meridian, 1966.

Pope Leo XIII. Encyclical, *Providentissimus Deus*, 1893.

Pope Pius XII. Encyclical, *Divino Afflante Spiritu*, 1943.

_____. Encyclical, *Humani Generis*, 1950.

Popper, Karl. *Conjectures and Refutations*. London, England: Routledge and Kegan Paul, 1963.

Pun, Pattle P.T. *Evolution, Nature and Scripture in Conflict?* Grand Rapids, Mich.: Zondervan Publishing House, 1982.

Rahner, Karl, S.J. *Hominization*. New York, N.Y.: Herder and Herder, 1965.

Reader, John. *Missing Links*. Boston, Mass.: Little, Brown and Company, 1981.

Rowbotham, Samuel (Parallax). *Zetetic Astronomy*. London, England: Simpkin, Marshall and Company, 1865.

Ruffini, Cardinal Ernesto. *The Theory of Evolution Judged by Reason and Faith*. New York, N.Y.: Wagner, 1959.

Ruse, Michael. *Darwinism Defended*. Reading, Mass.: Addison-Wesley, 1982.

Ryan, Bernard, F.S.C. *The Evolution of Man*. Westminster, Md.: The Newman Press, 1965.

Schadewald, Robert. "The Flat-out Truth," *Science Digest*, July 1980.

————. "The Evolution of Bible-science" in Godfrey, *Scientists Confront Creationism*. New York, N.Y.: W.W. Norton, 1983.

Sennot, Thomas Mary. *The Six Days of Creation*. Cambridge, Mass.: Ravengate Press, 1984.

Simpson, George Gaylord. *The Meaning of Evolution*. New Haven, Conn.: Yale University Press, 1949.

Slusher, Harold. *Critique of Radiometric Dating*. San Diego, Calif.: Institute for Creation Research, 1973.

Smith, Wolfgang. *Cosmos and Transcendence*. LaSalle, Ill.: Sherwood Sugden, 1984.

Stanley, Steven M. *The New Evolutionary Timetable*. New York, N.Y.: Basic Books, 1981.

Stravinskas, Peter. *The Catholic Response*. Huntington, Ind.: Our Sunday Visitor Publishing, 1985.

————. "The Errors of the New Catholic Fundamentalists," *Our Sunday Visitor*, May 26, 1985.

Tax, Sol, ed. *Evolution After Darwin*. Chicago, Ill.: Chicago University Press, 1960.

Taylor, F. Sherwood. *A Short History of Science and Scientific Thought*. New York: N.Y.: W.W. Norton, 1949.

Teilhard de Chardin, Pierre, S.J. *The Phenomenon of Man*. New York, N.Y.: Harper and Brothers, 1959.

Vawter, Bruce, C.M. *A Path Through Genesis*. New York, N.Y.: Sheed and Ward, 1956.

Whitcomb, John C. *The World That Perished*. Grand Rapids, Mich.: Baker Book House, 1973.

Williams, Rev. William. *Evolution of Man Scientifically Disproved in Fifty Arguments*. Camden, N.J.: W.A. Williams, 1928.

Wilson, Clifford, *In the Beginning God. . . .* Grand Rapids, Mich.: Baker Book House, 1975.

Wysong, R.L. *The Creation-Evolution Controversy*. Midland, Mich.: Inquiry Press, 1976.

Young, Davis A. *Christianity and the Age of the Earth*. Grand Rapids, Mich.: Zondervan Publishing House, 1982.

Index

165

166